COLORADO
MOUNTAIN CLUB
PACK GUIDE

I

COLORADO
SUMMIT
HIKES

SECOND EDITION

DAVE MULLER

The Colorado Mountain Club Press
Golden, Colorado

Colorado Summit Hikes, second edition
© 2018 by The Colorado Mountain Club

PUBLISHED BY

The Colorado Mountain Club Press
710 10th Street, Suite 200, Golden, CO 80401
303-996-2743   email: cmcpress@cmc.org
website: http://www.cmc.org

CONTACTING THE PUBLISHER:
We greatly appreciate when readers alert us to errors or outdated information by contacting us at cmcpress@cmc.org.

> Dave Muller: photographer unless noted otherwise
> Rebecca Finkel: book designer
> Mira Perrizo: copy editor
> Clyde Soles: publisher

COVER PHOTO: Mt. Neva by Dave Muller.

DISTRIBUTED TO THE BOOK TRADE BY:
Mountaineers Books, 1001 SW Klickitat Way, Suite 201,
Seattle, WA 98134, 800-553-4453, www.mountaineersbooks.org

We gratefully acknowledge the financial support of the people of Colorado through the Scientific and Cultural Facilities District of greater metropolitan Denver for our publishing activities.

TOPOGRAPHIC MAPS courtesy of CalTopo.com.

WARNING: Although there has been an effort to make the trail descriptions in this book as accurate as possible, some discrepancies may exist between the text and the trails in the field. Hiking in mountain areas is a high-risk activity. This guidebook is not a substitute for experience and common sense. The users of this guidebook assume full responsibility for their own safety. Weather, terrain conditions, and individual abilities must be considered before undertaking any of the hikes in this guide.

ISBN 978-1-937052-61-4

Printed in Korea

Opposite: Torreys Peak. (Nelson Chenkin)

Acknowledgment

So many people have helped in the production of this book. Besides the wonderful support of my wife, Jackie, and my family, thanks to my fellow hikers who comprise a weekly group known as The Seekers, and all those who have brought this book into print. These include the Colorado Mountain Club, Terry Root, Clyde Soles, Mira Perrizo, and Rebecca Finkel.

Above all, I thank the Great Intelligence, which gives us life, wonderful natural, and my cardiac pacemaker.

Contents

See pages 10 and 11 for a guide to the icons.

		Hike features	page
1	Genesee Mountain		24
2	Bald Mountain (Boulder County)		26
3	Ormes Peak		28
4	Mount Falcon	CMC CLASSIC HIKE	30
5	Fox Mountain	CMC CLASSIC HIKE	32
6	Mount Cutler	CMC CLASSIC HIKE	34
7	Alps Mountain		36
8	Squaw Mountain		38
9	St. Peters Dome		40
10	Cheesman Mountain		42
11	The Brother		44
12	Lichen Peak		46
13	Fairburn Mountain		48
14	Devils Head	CMC CLASSIC HIKE	50
15	Colorado Mines Peak		52
16	South Peak		54
17	Royal Mountain		56
18	Chief Mountain	CMC CLASSIC HIKE	58
19	Mount Zion and Colorow Hill		60
20	Fitzpatrick Peak		62
21	Emma Burr Mountain		64
22	Green Mountain	CMC CLASSIC HIKE	66
23	Lily Mountain		68
24	Douglas Mountain		70
25	Diamond Peaks		72
26	Mount Sniktau		74
27	Glacier Peak		76

How To Use This Guide

Each summit hike is rated as *easy, moderate, more difficult,* and *most difficult,* with background colors that correspond to the rating. Ratings are based on distance, elevation gain, and special challenges of the route. The hikes are presented in ascending degree of difficulty. When two peaks are listed for one hike, the rating applies to the difficulty in reaching both summits combined. Note that these ratings are highly subjective, and what may be easy for a seasoned hiker may be difficult for another. Start with a few easier summit hikes. After a few hikes, you should be able to get an idea of what level is right for you.

Easy **38**   Moderate **33**   More Difficult **28**   Most Difficult **3**

The **Hike Distance** shown is the mileage each way between the trailhead and the summit; in other words, the "one way" distance. Double this number to determine the round-trip distance for that outing. When there is a loop hike, with different ascent and descent routes, the two respective distances are given. If there is a hike with multiple destinations, then distances are given "point-to-point." In these latter cases then, just add all the distances for the total hiking distance.

Starting Elevation and **Elevation Gain** are self-explanatory. However, the latter is especially important in assessing the energy required for a summit hike. Sometimes, extra elevation gain is noted. This can occur if some elevation gain is lost, due to traveling through a dip or saddle, that must be re-gained; or if there is elevation gain required on a descent.

The time required for each hike, the **Hiking Time,** is divided into ascent and descent times and, when applicable, time necessary between two summits. These times were achieved by the author (at the time, a middle-aged, "peakbagger" in good condition) and only include moving time. A few hikes list Senior Time, which is for a spry octogenarian. Obviously, your times may be more or less, depending on your conditioning, your hiking habits, or the condition of the trail. You should use these times simply as a yardstick. After a few hikes, you should be able to determine whether to add or subtract any time for future planning.

The **Trail** listing takes note of how much of the hike, if any, is traveled on a trail. A trail is reassuring to most hikers, although some enjoy the greater feeling of adventure from off-trail travel. When there is bushwhacking involved in the hike, this is noted, often with a modifier such as "tundra and talus" or "some hand work or scrambling." Please note that, with the single exception of the last outing in this guide, there are no routes that involve extended rock scrambling.

The knowledge and use of map and compass, as well as attention to features of the terrain, are necessary skills for any of the hiking trips in this book, but are especially critical for bushwhacking. If you own a GPS receiver, you will want to establish several "waypoints" from the trailhead to the summit. These can be invaluable in navigating your return. Remember, dozens of people get lost in the Colorado Rockies each year. Don't be one of them.

The optimal time of the year for that hike is indicated by **Season**. On average, this is when the route is most likely to be free of snow. However, there is no such thing as an "average" year in the Rockies. Some winters are more severe and long lasting than others. Routes on south-facing slopes in years with less than average snowfall will often open up several weeks earlier than listed. Conversely, north-facing routes may stay snow-covered well into summer after a particularly severe winter. The first significant snowfall can occur as early as September or as late as November in the high country. The hiking season in Colorado is generally from early June through early October; but many of the peaks described in this guide, especially those at lower elevations, may be accessible over a longer period.

You can check with the management agency for the jurisdiction that contains your hike, in order to learn about the condition of your intended trail. Closures are not uncommon due to weather, fire or maintenance issues. You will find a list of management agencies and their addresses in the *Appendix*. Please take special notice when your intended hike enters a jurisdiction where special regulations are in force, such as a federally designated Wilderness Area.

Several types of relevant **Maps** are listed. Trails Illustrated maps now cover virtually all of western Colorado. They offer topographic features, good detail, and are weatherproof and tear-resistant. They are superior to USGS and USFS maps. A **Nearest Landmark** is provided to help narrow down your search for the trailhead.

On the trail beneath Capitol Peak. (David Hite)

Getting There

Directions to the trailheads are described from some close-by point of reference, such as a town, major highway or interchange. Obviously, the best way to get to somewhere is determined by where you start. Often, two different routes may be listed (for instance, from the north and from the south) but you may find another route more convenient. To the left of the description is an icon that graphically shows at a glance the condition of the access road to that trailhead. While there are very few hikes in this book that need a vehicle with four-wheel drive for access, there are several accesses on semi-rough, dirt roads that may become impassible to regular passenger cars during certain times, or be difficult in spots for low-clearance vehicles. If you have questions about road conditions, check with the management agency for that jurisdiction.

The text presents detailed descriptions for each hike. To minimize the chance for becoming lost or confused, special effort has been taken to give clear, unambiguous information about the route, without a lot of extraneous information. (But you will find a lot of useful, secondary information in the **Comments** section.) Emphasis is on distances, compass directions, and landmarks. In most cases, the word "trail" signifies a foot, bicycle, or stock route maintained by a management agency. In several cases, the word also applies to unmaintained "game" trails and to primitive roads. "Bushwhack" means to walk through forest, field or underbrush without benefit of trail. "Off-trail" is similar in meaning, but in this guide it applies to walking cross-country in open areas, such as above treeline. "Tundra" refers to the grassy landscape above treeline at higher elevations. "Scree" is a collection of small rocks and gravel on a mountainside, as opposed to "talus" which is a mass of rocks, ranging from fist-size to small boulders. A "couloir" refers to a narrow ravine on a steep mountainside. Finally, a "saddle" is a low point or pass between two summits or highpoints.

Hikes with Special Features or Outstanding Qualities

To the left of the hike description are symbols that convey additional information about special features or outstanding qualities of each hike. Many of these summit hikes are particularly ideal for special activities, such as wildlife or wildflower viewing, for families or persons with disabilities, or for hanging out with your canine companion. We also use symbols here to alert you when a hike shares a portion of the well-known Colorado Trail or the Continental Divide Trail, or if the hike enters a federally designated Wilderness Area, where special use regulations may apply. Some of these summits are even great for mountain bicyclists looking for a challenging ride or for trail runners. You will find a complete Legend describing all the symbols used for identifying special hikes on the facing page. The special characteristics of each hike are also listed in the Table of Contents.

Icons

 CMC Classic: Some of these summit hikes have become favorites of the Colorado Mountain Club, which are enjoyed year after year. We highly recommend these hikes because of their outstanding scenic or wilderness qualities—or because they are just plain fun! But remember, the most rewarding classics are the ones that you discover yourself.

 Family Hikes: This symbol indicates a good hike for families with small children, for hikers with limited mobility, or for seniors who are looking for a less-strenuous hike. These summit hikes are short with modest elevation gain and on well-maintained trails. All of them are in the "Green" section (portion of the book with easier hikes).

 Wildlife Hikes: Here we indicate hikes where you have a good chance of viewing some of our spectacular Rocky Mountain wildlife. Wildlife viewing is possible on any hike in this book; but in the text for these hikes, we indicate some unique or better-than-average opportunities. You can increase you chances of viewing animals on any hike by being out early or late in the day.

 Wildflower Hikes: The Colorado Rockies are justifiably famous for spectacular displays of summer wildflowers. Many of the hikes in this book are excellent for viewing plants in all three encountered life zones. But the hikes indicated here are especially wonderful, with many species represented in large numbers. Peak times are early May (foothills) to early July (high peaks).

Dog Hikes: This symbol shows hikes that you may enjoy sharing with your canine companion. Few of the hikes in this book restrict dogs; but we have tried to choose outings where dogs typically are welcome and common. Dogs have varying abilities, just like people. We have picked hikes that have good trails suitable for most dogs. Remember to keep your dog leashed and under control.

Trail Running: Trail running in the mountains is a popular sport, particularly around the urban centers of the Front Range. We have picked out a handful of good ones that are recommended by enthusiasts. Since most people are not ultra-marathoners or long-distance runners, we have chosen short to moderate runs on good trails with modest gradients.

Geology/Geography Hikes: The Colorado Rockies have been shaped by complex forces over millions of years. Every hike in this book has a fascinating story to tell in its rocks and landforms. We have only picked a handful of hikes that have something truly interesting about them.

Fall Hikes: Autumn in the high country is a magical time, as aspen leaves change to golden hues and the tundra becomes a soft carpet of muted reds. We indicate hikes here that will delight your senses and consume rolls of film! The fall season is short—from early September to early October—with peak times varying from year to year depending on the weather.

Bike Trips: Mountain bicycling is enormously popular in Colorado. Some of the summit hikes in this guide are suitable for bike rides. Riders should be experienced with riding on single tracks with steep grades. Remember that bikes aren't allowed in designated Wilderness Areas.

Fee Areas: This symbol alerts you when a hike enters a managed area where fees are charged for day use. This is becoming more common, especially with so-called "demonstration projects" in certain National Forest areas. State and National Parks also typically have entrance fees.

Wilderness Area: This symbol indicates that a portion of this hike is in a federally designated Wilderness Area where special regulations typically apply.

Colorado Trail: The familiar Colorado Trail symbol is used to indicate a hike that shares a segment of the popular 468-mile trail between Denver and Durango.

Continental Divide Trail: This symbol means that a portion of the hike is along the Continental Divide National Scenic Trail. Note that this trail is not always right on the Divide, but often follows existing trails that parallel the Divide. The Colorado portion of this trail is about 750 miles long.

Using Peak Finder

One of the great pleasures of standing atop a Colorado summit is in identifying for yourself and friends the many peaks around you. **Peak Finder** can help. It shows the approximate position of neighboring peaks by compass direction relative to the summit you are on. Your summit is located by GPS coordinates, expressed as latitude and longitude, in the center of the Peak Finder circle.

Hiking Colorado's Summits

Colorado's Rocky Mountains form a spectacular roof, capping the western United States. With 54 peaks over 14,000 feet high, over 1,500 others that extend above timberline, and nearly 4,000 individual summits in all, Colorado offers an alpine playground with some of the best hiking and climbing opportunities in the world.

Excellent access to this mountain paradise is courtesy of a maze of developed roads and trails that reach the most scenic areas. Yet, Colorado's mountains still contain wild and pristine places that will thrill any backcountry user.

Starting up Chief Mountain. (Terry Root)

This guide describes 102 hikes with 113 summits that explore some of the best that the Colorado Rockies has to offer. Many have either not appeared before in other guides, or have lacked certain details or emphasis that the author considers important. With the tremendous interest in hiking and climbing summits in Colorado, special care has been made to avoid some peaks that are overly popular. Instead, you will get to know for yourself many lesser-known and uncrowded gems, hopefully experiencing the same sense of discovery as the author. These routes are intended for a wide variety of hikers with different skill and experience levels. The beginning hiker, the newcomer to Colorado, families with children, those with certain physical limitations, and even the advanced hiker will all find routes of interest in this guidebook.

None of the hikes require special technical ability or equipment. The routes cover peaks ranging from 6,000 feet to over 14,000 feet in height and are situated throughout the vast topography of the Colorado mountains. Users of this guide, who reach even just a sampling of the varied summits, will nonetheless come away with a deep appreciation of the splendor and majesty of the Colorado Rockies.

Mountain Geography

While the Colorado mountains have been divided into dozens of individual ranges, they are commonly divided into six main geographic sections or groups, listed from east to west: the *Front Range,* the *Sangre de Cristo Mountains,* the *Park Range* (including familiar sub-units of the Park, Gore, Tenmile and Mosquito Ranges), the *Sawatch Range,* the *Elk Mountains,* and the *San Juan Mountains.* Most of these groups run in a general north-south direction, with exceptions being the Elk Mountains that trend west and east and the expansive jumble of the San Juan Mountains. The *Continental*

Above treeline. (Eric Wiseman)

Divide winds through these ranges for nearly 700 miles, creating headwaters for many of the nation's major river systems and effectively dividing the state and its communities into the "Western Slope" and the "Eastern Slope." Looking at the map on page 22, note that this guide contains summit hikes in all of the six major ranges and on both "slopes" of the Divide.

Mountain Climate and Weather

Within the huge elevation gradient that exists in the mountains of Colorado, climate is relative to location. A warm, sunny day in the foothills may present near winter-like conditions on the high peaks. Even in one location, mountain weather can be unpredictable, with large temperature swings throughout the day, or as Coloradans are wont to say, "If you don't like the weather, wait ten minutes."

None of the summit hikes in this guide are described as winter outings. We can make some general observations about what you might expect from the remaining three seasons. In **spring,** the high peaks are still gripped with snow, with most hiking opportunities occurring on the foothill peaks, especially those with southern exposures. March through May can be comfortably warm, but often can be windy as well. Sudden spring storms can dump fresh snow on the mountains, closing off access to even the lowest peaks in the foothills for a few days. The arrival of **summer** brings low humidity, sunny mornings, stormy afternoons, and clear nights to the Colorado high country. From July through August, warm (and even hot) conditions prevail, offering access to even the highest summits in this guide. It is critical to get an early start on your hike, as severe local thunderstorms typically rack the mountains on

Approaching storm—get down off the ridge! (Terry Root)

Aspen leaves along Horse Creek. (Steve Waterman)

most afternoons. While brief and fast moving, these storms contain high winds, rain or hail, and dangerous lightning. **Autumn,** though heartbreakingly short in the high country, can be the best time of all to experience many of the summit hikes in this book. Days are crystal clear with less chance of late-day storms, while nights are quite crisp. The quaking aspen turn ablaze and the tundra is carpeted with rich, fall colors. During this less-crowded time of year, the mountain world seems to pause and reflect before the first snow falls in early October. Soon the storms arrive in earnest, closing off the high peaks for another year; but many of the foothill summits in this guide can be enjoyed for several more weeks.

Mountain Geology

Pikes Peak granite on Bison Peak. (Terry Root)

The present-day Rockies began to take shape about 70 million years ago, during a massive uplift called the Laramide orogeny. After a long period of erosion reduced these ancestral Rockies to mostly rubble, a second period of mountain building began about 26 million years ago, pushing the peaks close to their present height. An intense period of glaciation over several thousand years, ending only recently in geologic time, helped shape and scour the landscape to the forms that we see today. The several processes involved in creating the Rockies have resulted in many rock types to be found on the summit hikes in this guide, including examples of the three main classifications: *igneous, sedimentary,* and *metamorphic.* Hiking up these summits, you will also discover interesting landforms and features that result from both the recent and ancient geologic past—glacial cirques, alpine lakes, fault-block ranges, and unusual minerals, including the gold and silver bearing deposits that fed Colorado's great mining era.

Mountain Life Zones

The Colorado summits described in this book range in elevation from foothill peaks that are shoved up against the Plains at 6,800 feet, to the highest peaks in the Rockies at over 14,000 feet, providing the summit hiker with a remarkable variety of habitats to experience and enjoy. Three *life* zones are represented on these summits, each with characteristic plants and animals.

The **Foothills** begin at the edge of the Plains' grasslands and range to an elevation of about 9,000 feet. Summits here typically have fine, open stands of ponderosa pine on their south-facing slopes, with dense forests of Douglas fir on their northern exposures. A thick riparian forest flourishes along rivers and streams, supporting numerous bird species. Beaver, porcupine, skunk, and fox are common, with herds of mule deer and elk as winter migrants. The hiker on a foothill summit will be eye-to-eye with red-tailed hawks, climbing thermals from more than a thousand feet below.

The **Subalpine,** between elevations of 9,000 to 11,000 feet, is a rich and varied environment with dominant forests of Engelmann spruce and subalpine fir. The dark, shady spruce-fir forests support more solitary-like animals such as black bear, moose, mountain lion, and lynx. In higher forests, ancient and wind blasted bristlecone pine and limber pine replace the spruce-fir forest near timberline. Burned-over areas soon become clothed with fast-growing aspen or lodgepole pine. Aspen groves are very rich in life with abundant bird species, as well as mule deer and elk. The understory is open

Ypsilon Mountain

enough to harbor showy displays of summer wildflowers. Summit hikers, pausing for lunch on one of these subalpine peaks, will likely soon meet the gray jay, or camp robber.

At about 11,000 feet, the cold and wind begin to preclude upright trees, producing stunted versions, shaped by those elements of the high Alpine. Above that, the trees give way to tundra that holds a wide variety of habitats, including nearly impenetrable willow stands, rocky and gravelly areas with scattered cushion plants, fell fields of boulders, snowbeds with meltwater bogs beneath, and lush meadows of tussock grasses. Hugging the ground are hardy alpine wildflowers, sharing this harsh landscape with interesting animal species, among them marmot, pika, and white-tailed ptarmigan. Lucky summit hikers in the alpine may spot magnificent bighorn sheep silhouetted along a high ridge, or mountain goats patrolling the ledges of a steep cliff face.

Endless possibilities. (Terry Root)

Safety On the Hike

Although the Colorado Rockies generally are one of the safest mountain environments in North America, any book of hiking routes cannot free the user from the need for good judgment. There are dangers in the backcountry that every hiker needs to be aware of. Each year, serious injuries and deaths occur in the Colorado backcountry—despite most accidents being preventable. Even a minor fall on rock can be injurious and weather conditions can change rapidly, transforming an easy route into a difficult one.

Abandoned Mines The Colorado mountains are littered with long-abandoned mine shafts and old workings. Some of the charm of the hikes in this guide is due to these fascinating, historic sites. In addition to being inherently unstable, mines may still harbor poisonous gasses or caustic materials. Old buildings and workings often lean precariously, ready to collapse at a touch. Take photos, marvel at the tenacity of the old pioneers, but stay out!

Altitude Sickness Hiking up summits in this guide will take you to elevations ranging from a modest 6,000 feet, to a headache inducing 14,000 feet. Every hiker will react differently to the effects of altitude. Acute Mountain Sickness (AMS), is caused by a lack of oxygen when traveling to higher elevations. This usually occurs in individuals exposed to an altitude over

The old Urad Mine. (Terry Root)

7,000 feet who have not had a chance to acclimate to the altitude before engaging in physical activities. The symptoms of AMS include, but are not limited to, headache, nausea, vomiting, and shortness of breath. Drinking plenty of fluids and ascending at a reasonable rate will help to offset the potential of being afflicted with AMS. If you do get AMS, the best advice is to descend immediately to a lower altitude. Untreated, altitude sickness can be fatal.

Avalanche Awareness Avalanches are, for the most part, a winter phenomenon, which will not be a consideration on most of the hikes in this book. However, avalanches do still occur in late spring and early summer on the high peaks. Avoid walking out on cornices or climbing up steep couloirs that might break and run on a

Horseshoe Mountain earned it's name from the distinctive east face. (Terry Root)

warm afternoon. Take an *Avalanche Awareness* course, offered by several recreational organizations including the Colorado Mountain Club, to learn how to judge danger in the snowpack.

Hypothermia Hypothermia occurs when the internal core body temperature drops to dangerous levels after exposure to cold and wetness. With the quick changing weather patterns typical of high mountains, this is a real danger in Colorado, even in summer—hypothermia can kill. Symptoms are slurred speech, irrational behavior, drowsiness, and intense shivering. Keep warm and dry, carry spare clothing, and respond quickly to rain and wind by donning appropriate clothing. Treat a victim by replacing wet clothing with dry, by providing warm drinks and high-energy foods, and by huddling for shared body warmth.

Lightning Deadly lightning is always a threat when thunderstorms are present. Afternoon thunderstorms are fairly common during the summer in Colorado, especially on the high peaks. These storms are quick moving and brief, but can be very violent. Lightning normally strikes the highest features in the vicinity—that could be YOU, if you are on a summit or a high ridge. Head down from any highpoint immediately when you see a thunderstorm starting to materialize. If caught in a place threatened by a strike, crouch down in a depression, with a pack or article of clothing to insulate you from potential ground currents, and discard any metal objects, such as an ice axe.

Rock Fall Scree and talus fields can potentially pose a danger to hikers from rock falls. This is actually one of the most common accidents, especially occurring in narrow gullies and couloirs. Even just a fist-size rock can strike with amazing velocity, seriously injuring a climber. Spread out laterally in a couloir to prevent one person from being in "the line of fire" of another. Test handholds and footholds in scrambling situations and wear a helmet specifically designed for climbing.

Sun Exposure At higher elevations ultraviolet rays (UVRs) are approximately 50 to 60 percent stronger than at sea level. Therefore, sunburn can occur more quickly and severely at altitude, especially in snowy terrain where the sunlight is reflected back up by the snow. UVRs can also penetrate cloud cover—so that even on cool, overcast days, you can be at risk. Apply sunscreen to all exposed skin areas one hour prior to sun exposure. This gives the sunscreen time to penetrate the deeper skin layers. Sunscreen that is rated SPF 30 is the suggested standard for extended outdoor exposure. Look for sunscreens that block both UVA and UVB rays. Don't forget to protect your eyes with sunglasses that are rated to block both types of UVRs.

Water Treat any water taken from unprotected sources before you drink it, and practice proper hygiene. You are at risk from Giardia contamination anytime you drink from untreated water sources in the Colorado backcountry. *Giardia* is a microscopic organism that, once it has inhabited the digestive system, can cause severe diarrhea. Giardia is mainly spread by the activity of animals in the watershed area of the water supply, or by the introduction of sewage into the water supply.

Giardia has become so common, even in wilderness areas, that water should always be treated chemically with pills that are specifically designed for water purification, by filtering the water with an approved water filter, or by boiling untreated water before using.

Rushing Rock Creek. (Terry Root)

Wildlife Encounters While most hikers don't perceive wildlife as a threat to them, serious encounters with aggressive animals are on the rise in Colorado. Most problems center around food. Don't feed wildlife, and be sure to hang your food out of reach when in the backcountry. Any large animal should be treated

cautiously, but bears, moose, and mountain lions are the main concern. Hiking at dawn or dusk may increase your chances of meeting a bear or mountain lion. Use extra caution in places where hearing or visibility is limited: in brushy areas, near streams, where trails round a bend, or on windy days. Avoid hiking alone and keep small children close and in sight. Fortunately, both bears and moun-

Mountain goats on Buffalo Mountain. (Eric Wiseman) tain lions are reclusive creatures that still largely have a healthy fear of humans in unpopulated areas. Moose are notoriously ill-tempered, particularly when dogs are present, and should be given a wide berth.

Staying Found Be prepared for the backcountry with a good map, a compass, and orienteering skills. It is not advised to hike alone; but if you do so, make sure to leave plans with someone—including information about your trailhead, your destination, and your date of return.

Self-rescue should be the first consideration in the case of illness or an accident on a hike. If it is deemed necessary to seek outside help, someone should stay with the injured person; or failing that, then leave warm clothing, food and water behind. Purchase a *Colorado Outdoor Recreation Search and Rescue Card,* offered by the state of Colorado and available at outdoor retailers or sporting goods stores. This helps cover the cost of search and rescue in Colorado.

Clothing and Equipment When preparing for a hike, always start with the *Ten Essentials* as your foundation. Boots should be light but sturdy (no running shoes). Backpackers will want heavier, stiffer boots for good support. For clothing, modern synthetics are light, insulate well, and dry quickly. But merino wool clothing is still effective, even when damp. Avoid cotton entirely, as it loses

The 10 Essentials
Food
Water
Emergency shelter
Extra clothing
First aid kit
Flashlight
Map and compass
Matches/fire starter
Pocketknife
Sunglasses/sunscreen

all insulating ability when wet. Effective, good-quality clothing and other gear will often determine the difference between a safe, enjoyable day in the mountains and an unpleasant, or even potentially disastrous, experience.

Wilderness Responsibilities

The hikes in this guide traverse a number of publicly managed land units, including several National Forests, one National Park, Colorado State Park lands, and several parks under local control by counties or cities. Please be aware that private land often abuts these units. Respect any private property and "no trespassing" postings. Remember also that federal law protects cultural and historic sites on public lands, such as old cabins, mines, and Indian sites. These historic cultural assets are important to us all as a society, and are not meant to be scavenged for personal gain.

Forest Service occupancy regulations are primarily designed to limit wear and tear in fragile wilderness areas. However, even non-wilderness areas need to be treated lightly to preserve resources for future generations. Strive to leave no trace of your passing.

Before starting your hike, check with the Forest Service for the current forest fire danger, which can sometimes be extreme, and for any restrictions on campfires. A list of contact addresses for Forest Service offices and the offices of other publicly managed lands is provided at the back of this book.

Wilderness Areas

In this guide, we alert you to hikes that enter any federally designated Wilderness Area. The Wilderness Act of 1964 prohibits logging, mining, permanent structures, commercial enterprises, and motorized/mechanical transport in these protected areas. Minimize impact on these pristine and spectacular places by following these rules:

1. Camp at least 200 feet from lakes and streams.
2. Use a stove rather than building a fire.
3. Bury human waste six inches deep and 200 feet from water sources.
4. Pack out toilet paper.
5. All dogs must be leashed (or are prohibited in some areas).
6. Pack out your trash.
7. Mountain biking is prohibited.

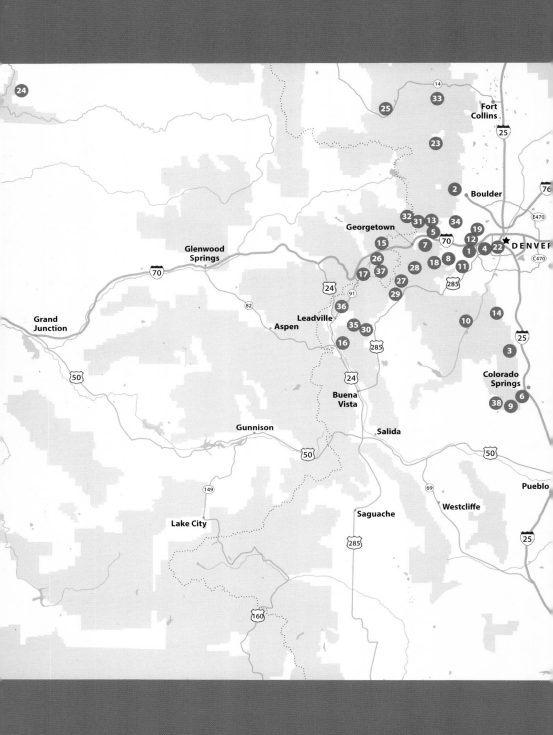

1 Genesee Mountain 8,284 Feet

DISTANCE: 0.4 mile each way

STARTING ELEVATION: 7,980 feet

ELEVATION GAIN: 304 feet

HIKING TIME: Up in 12 minutes, down in 8 minutes

TRAIL: All the way

SEASON: Early April to early November

MAPS: Trails Illustrated #100

NEAREST LANDMARK: Denver

GETTING THERE: From I-70 at Exit #254, 20 miles west of Denver, cross south over the highway. Turn right after 60 yards from the overpass onto Genesee Mountain Road and go for 1.1 miles from Interstate 70 and park in the open area on the right.

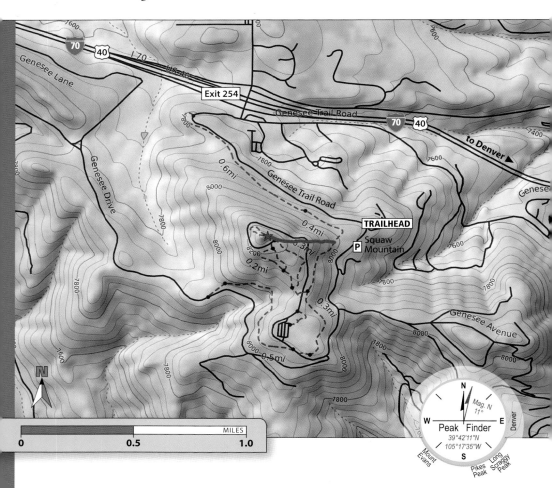

Looking west to Mount Evans.

COMMENTS: This hike lies within an area designated as a Denver Mountain Park, part of one of the largest urban park systems in the country. Begun in 1912 with the acquisition of Genesee, the system now has 31 named properties on 14,000 acres of mountains and foothills.

A group of buffalo graze in a large enclosure on the north flank of Genesee Mountain. The herd was started with seven animals that were shipped by rail from Yellowstone at around the time of the First World War. Both buffalo and an elk herd can be viewed year-round by the public.

A local group of the Daughters of the American Revolution has placed a new flag on the summit flagpole on every Flag Day since 1911.

THE ROUTE: Begin southwest on a trail that quickly curves right at a fork. Reach a road crossing and ascend northwest. Cross a parking area and rise to the summit flagpole and benchmark. Return to the east-southeast, on the same route as you ascended. Be on the lookout for beautiful, cup-shaped pasque flowers that commonly dot these slopes in early spring.

2 Bald Mountain (Boulder County) 7,160 feet

DISTANCE: 0.5 mile each way (loop)

STARTING ELEVATION: 6,960 feet

ELEVATION GAIN: 220 feet (includes an extra 20 feet of elevation loss on the ascent)

HIKING TIME: Up in 14 minutes, down in 8 minutes

TRAIL: All the way

SEASON: May until late October

MAPS: Trails Illustrated #100; City of Boulder Open Space Trails Map; Bald Mountain Scenic Area Map

NEAREST LANDMARK: Boulder

GETTING THERE: From Broadway in central Boulder, drive west on Mapleton Avenue (which becomes Boulder County 52 and the Sunshine Canyon Road) for 5.0 miles to a parking area and a Bald Mountain sign on the left.

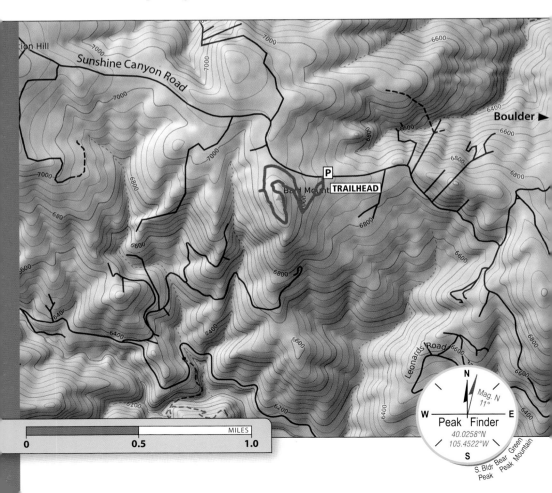

COMMENTS: This small parcel of Boulder County Open Space provides an ideal summit trail for young children or those with some physical limitations. A good vista is available from the easily accessible top. Several primitive benches are along the trail. There are two picnic tables and a toilet near the trailhead.

THE ROUTE: Enter through a gate and follow the loop trail to the southwest and counterclockwise to a bench and a few trees at the top. Continue your descent to the northwest and in five minutes reach a "T." Go left past picnic tables to complete the loop at the trailhead.

This is mostly an open hike with some ponderosa trees and nice views at the top. (Terry Root)

3 Ormes Peak 9,727 Feet

DISTANCE: 0.3 mile each way

STARTING ELEVATION: 9,320 feet

ELEVATION GAIN: 407 feet

HIKING TIME: Up in 22 minutes, down in 8 minutes

TRAIL: Intermittent and faint

SEASON: Early May to late October

MAPS: Trails Illustrated #137

NEAREST LANDMARK: Colorado Springs

GETTING THERE: From Colorado Springs, drive northwest from I-25 on US-24 for 17.8 miles to the town of Woodland Park. At Baldwin Street, where a sign welcomes the visitor to Woodland Park, turn right (northwest). Baldwin becomes a street called Rampart Range Road (and also Teller County Road 22). Take this

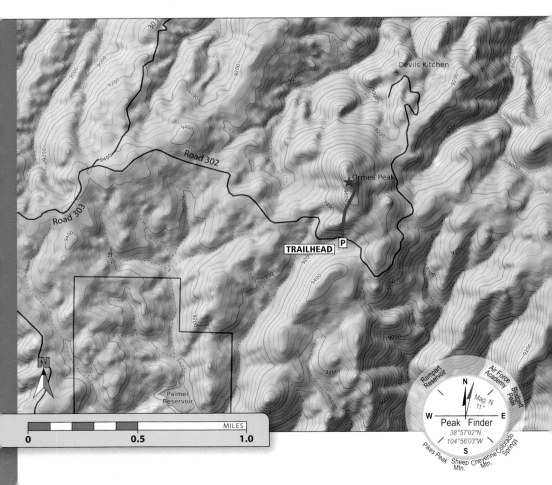

road for 2.95 miles from US-24, to an intersection with Loy Creek Road. Turn right on Loy Creek Road and ascend the canyon for 1.5 miles to a four-way intersection. Turn right (south) onto the *real* Rampart Range Road, which is unpaved. Go southwest on Rampart Range Road for 6.1 miles to a turnoff to the east, which is Road 303. Follow this road east for 0.95 mile to another fork. Take the right fork, which is Road 302. Take this road east for 1.35 miles and park off the road on the left (north).

From the south, access is via Rampart Range Road, which begins in the southwest corner of the Garden of the Gods, 0.1 mile east of Balanced Rock. To reach the turnoff onto Road 303, drive north on Rampart Range Road for 15.15 miles. The last mile or so (on Road 302) can be deeply rutted, so a vehicle with adequate clearance is recommended.

COMMENTS: This mountain is named after Manley Ormes, the father of Robert M. Ormes, who was the original editor of the frequently revised *Guide to the Colorado Mountains,* in continuous publication for half a century. The elder Ormes mapped some of the area and helped found the Saturday Knights, a group that hiked every Saturday in the Pikes Peak area.

THE ROUTE: Proceed up and due north through the sparse trees. A faint trail is intermittent to the top, but the hike is easily done without any trail. The unmarked summit lies at the northwestern edge of a relatively flat area. The view of Pikes Peak from here is extraordinary. Return by the ascent route.

Ormes Peak from the south. (Eric Wiseman)

4 Mount Falcon 7,851 Feet

DISTANCE: 0.66 mile each way

STARTING ELEVATION: 7,780 feet

ELEVATION GAIN: 231 feet (includes 80 feet extra each way)

HIKING TIME: Up in 20 minutes, down in 15 minutes

TRAIL: All the way

SEASON: Early April to late November

MAPS: Trails Illustrated #100; Mount Falcon Park Map (Jefferson County Open Space)

NEAREST LANDMARK: Kittredge

GETTING THERE: Either drive south from CO-74 at Kittredge on Meyers Gulch Road for 2.9 miles, or drive north from US-285 on Parmalee Gulch Road for 2.75 miles. (Parmalee Gulch Road goes north from US-285 in Turkey Creek Canyon, east of Conifer and west of the Evergreen cutoff. This road becomes Meyers Gulch Road before it reaches CO-74.) Turn east on Picutis Road and

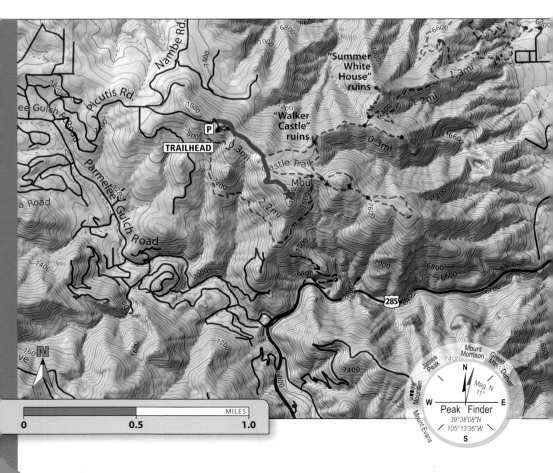

The ruins of "Walker's Castle."

make a quick left turn onto Comanche Road. After 0.1 mile, turn right onto Oh Kay Road and after another 0.1 mile, turn right onto Picutis Road. After 0.45 mile, turn left onto Nambe Road and drive 1.3 miles farther to road end at the Mount Falcon Park parking area.

COMMENTS: Mount Falcon was named by John Brisben Walker, a successful entrepreneur who died in 1931 at the age of 84. Walker had a Doctor of Philosophy degree from Georgetown University in Washington, D.C. He brought *Cosmopolitan* magazine into prominence and established nearby Red Rocks Park. He hoped to build a mansion for himself, as well as a summer White House for the President near the top of Mount Falcon. The home's ruins are located 0.5 mile north of the summit and the summer White House ruins are 1.0 mile northeast of the summit tower. Both can be reached easily by trail.

THE ROUTE: The well-marked trailhead is evident at the southeastern corner of the parking area. Continue southeast past picnic tables and toilet facilities for 0.3 mile to a fork. Turn right and continue to the south on the Tower Trail, which also leads to the Eagles Eye Shelter. In another 0.1 mile on the Tower Trail, there is another fork. Keep right and stay on the Tower Trail, ascend some stone steps, and in 0.26 mile, the summit and overlying, wooden lookout tower are reached. The most direct descent route is to backtrack on the route just described. However, if you wish to take a longer loop trail back to your vehicle, and perhaps explore the park further, there are several possible trails on the Mount Falcon Park map.

5 Fox Mountain 10,921 Feet

DISTANCE: 0.65 mile each way

STARTING ELEVATION: 10,470 feet

ELEVATION GAIN: 451 feet

HIKING TIME: Up in 25 minutes, down in 15 minutes

TRAIL: To St. Marys Lake, off-trail beyond the lake

SEASON: Late May to early October

MAPS: Trails Illustrated #103

NEAREST LANDMARK: Idaho Springs

GETTING THERE: Drive west of Idaho Springs on I-70 for about 2 miles and turn off on Exit #238. Go north on Fall River Road (which is designated Road 275) for 9.1 miles, past fee parking areas on the left, to a right-turning curve off the paved road. Take the dirt road on the left at a "No Parking" sign and after 0.2 mile, park

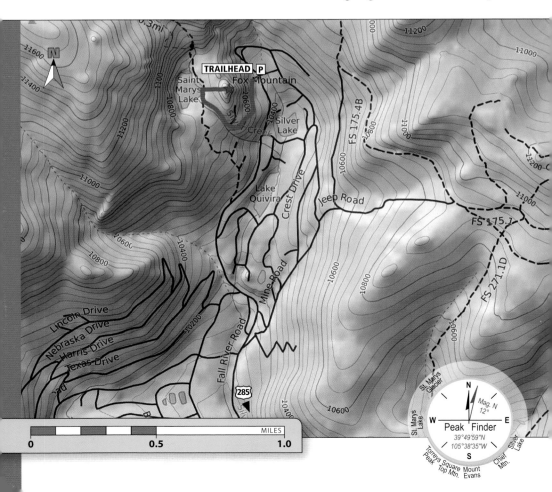

off the road at a four-way intersection. There are no signs to prohibit parking at this junction.

COMMENTS: St. Marys Glacier is located above the north end of St. Marys Lake. It is actually an icefield rather than a true glacier and sits at the bottom of a natural funnel. During the winter, snow blows down from the Continental Divide and is swept into this narrow valley, collecting into an area approximately ten acres wide. In most years, this snow never completely melts. However in 2002, after three years of severe drought in the area, the "glacier" nearly disappeared, revealing an assortment of long-lost, oddball items, from broken skis, to an engine block, to a recliner!

With a *nearly* permanent snowfield so easily accessible, St. Marys Glacier is very popular with summer skiers and snowboarders. Organizations, like the Colorado Mountain Club, regularly conduct classes here that train in mountaineering skills.

THE ROUTE: From the four-way intersection, proceed south up an old mining road for about ten minutes to a bend in the road toward the north. Follow a trail that passes to the west, on the north side of the creek. In another seven minutes, you will arrive at St. Marys Lake. From the eastern margin of the lake, leave the trail and bushwhack east, up over mostly talus, to the top of Fox Mountain. Some easy handwork is necessary near the summit, which consists of three rocky knobs on a rocky mesa. Descend via the ascent route.

CMC
CLASSIC
HIKE

Nearing the summit of Fox Mountain. (Linda Grey)

6

Mount Cutler 7,200 Feet

DISTANCE: 1.0 mile each way

STARTING ELEVATION: 6,785 feet

ELEVATION GAIN: 427 feet (includes 31 feet extra each way)

HIKING TIME: Up in 23 minutes, down in 20 minutes

TRAIL: All the way

SEASON: Early April through late November

MAPS: Trails Illustrated #137; North Cheyenne Cañon Park Map (Colorado Springs Park and Recreation Department)

NEAREST LANDMARK: Colorado Springs

GETTING THERE: At the southern part of Colorado Springs, from I-25, and take Exit #140B onto South Tejon Street. Go 0.4 mile then turn right on Cheyenne Boulevard and proceed southwest for 2.5 miles to an intersection with Evans

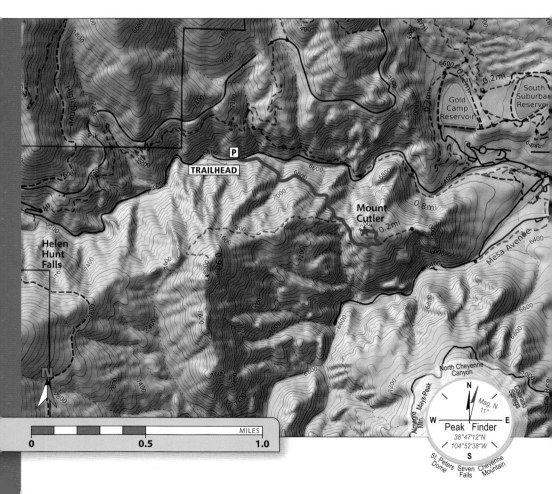

Avenue, close to the entrance to Seven Falls (fee area) and a sign marking the beginning of North Cheyenne Canyon. Drive up the scenic, paved North Cheyenne Canyon Road for 1.5 miles to a parking area on the left (south) side of the road and a Mount Cutler trail sign. Park here.

Cheyenne Mountain from the summit of Mount Cutler.

COMMENTS: This mountain is named after Henry Cutler, a Massachusetts man who gave large amounts of money to Colorado College in its early years.

The hiking area lies within North Cheyenne Cañon Park, part of the city of Colorado Springs park system. Close-in to the city with easy access, nearly 70,000 visitors a year enjoy the towering evergreens, interesting rock formations, and scenic waterfalls of this 1,000-foot deep gorge, which cuts through ancient Pikes Peak granite. Several other trails and picnic areas can also be found within the 1,600-acre park. This particular hike will usually be free of snow and ice between April and November.

THE ROUTE: Follow the clear trail, up and southeast, as it curls to the unmarked, tree-covered top of Mount Cutler. En route to the top, there are good overlooks of Seven Falls to the south. Descend as you came up.

7 Alps Mountain 10,560 Feet

DISTANCE: 0.45 mile each way

STARTING ELEVATION: 9,940 feet

ELEVATION GAIN: 620 feet

HIKING TIME: Up in 30 minutes, down in 26 minutes

TRAIL: Initial 0.3 mile, bushwhack beyond

SEASON: Early June to early October

MAPS: Trails Illustrated #104

NEAREST LANDMARK: Idaho Springs

GETTING THERE: From I-70 in Idaho Springs, drive southwest on CO-103 for 0.5 mile. Turn right onto unpaved Spring Gulch Road and ascend 4.3 miles to a four-way intersection and park your vehicle. En route to this point, drive parallel to the small creek on your left. Keep right at mile 1.6, left at mile 1.75, straight at

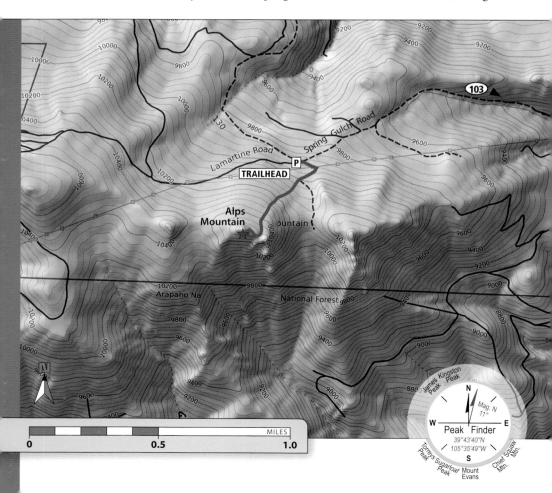

mile 2.1 and again at mile 2.5, left at mile 2.6, right at mile 3.0 and again at mile 3.9, left at mile 4.0 and again left at mile 4.1. Regular cars can reach this trailhead.

COMMENTS: From the summit of Alps Mountain, the terrain drops steeply down into the canyon of Chicago Creek. It was along the banks of this stream, near present-day Idaho Springs, that George Jackson discovered placer gold in January of 1859. The ensuing rush pushed miners into the surrounding hills, searching for the load. As a result, the area of this hike is honeycombed with old mines and their roads.

This is a good outing for beginners or for early season conditioning. The route should be free of snow at least between June and October.

Alps Mountain drops steeply on its east side into Chicago Creek.

THE ROUTE: Proceed southeast up the road on your left. The road curves south and in 0.25 mile you will arrive at a restored, old cabin. Take the left fork above the cabin and continue southwest and west. Thirty yards past the cabin, take a left fork to the west-southwest, just before some mine remnants. The trail ends in a loop within forty yards. Then bushwhack southwest past some diggings, with an abandoned cabin on your left. Ascend west on a faint trail and then curve southwest to reach the unmarked, rocky summit at the west end of an irregular ridge. The views from the top are partially obscured by trees. Return as you ascended.

8 Squaw Mountain 11,486 Feet

DISTANCE: 0.6 mile each way

STARTING ELEVATION: 10,960 feet

ELEVATION GAIN: 526 feet

HIKING TIME: Up in 27 minutes, down in 21 minutes

TRAIL: All the way

SEASON: Mid-May to mid-October

MAPS: Trails Illustrated #100

NEAREST LANDMARK: Idaho Springs

GETTING THERE: Drive south on CO-74 from Exit 252 of I-70. After 3.3 miles, turn west on CO-103 (Squaw Pass Road) and go 12.0 miles, then turn left (southeast) on a dirt road. Drive mostly east and up on this road, until a barrier blocks further vehicular traffic after 0.9 mile from CO-103. Park off the road.

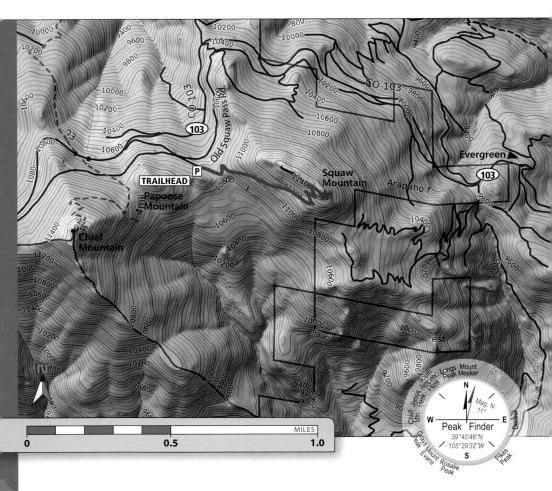

Approaching the lookout tower on the summit of Squaw Mountain. (Terry Root)

COMMENTS: Squaw Mountain, with its bare area on the north flank, can usually be clearly seen from Denver. The summit is easily accessible and affords excellent vistas from its historic lookout tower.

The first lookout on the site was put up in the 1920s by the city of Denver. In 1940, the present, more permanent structure was built of wood and stone by the Civilian Conservation Corps. It was still in service until the late 1980s, then was restored recently by the Forest Service and placed on the National Historic Lookout Register.

It is being considered for re-staffing again to help in fire detection because of the tremendous growth of expensive homes just outside the National Forest. Unfortunately, the site is also being sought for further expansion of the existing radio and TV antenna facilities.

THE ROUTE: Proceed northeast on the road past the barrier. The road makes several curves as it ascends. Take the right fork in the road near the top and hike directly toward the lookout tower. A good trail begins at a wooden pole at the edge of a turnaround area at road end. Take the trail northeast, and then east, for the last 300 feet to the summit lookout tower. Descend by the same route.

9 St. Peters Dome 9,690 Feet

DISTANCE: 0.8 mile each way

STARTING ELEVATION: 9,278 feet

ELEVATION GAIN: 542 feet (includes 65 extra feet each way)

HIKING TIME: Up in 28 minutes, down in 21 minutes

TRAIL: Most of the way, vague around the top

SEASON: Early May to early November

MAPS: Trails Illustrated #137

NEAREST LANDMARK: Colorado Springs

GETTING THERE: From I-25 in southern Colorado Springs, drive south on Nevada Avenue (which becomes CO-115) for 1.8 miles and turn right on Cheyenne Mountain Boulevard. Follow this road around a circle and past various intersections for 2.4 miles to the intersection with Cheyenne Mountain Zoo Road. Continue

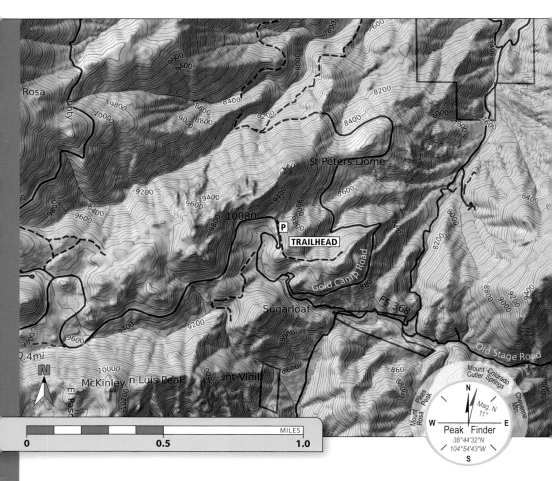

The summit of St. Peters Dome with Colorado Springs far below.

straight onto Old Stage Road for 6.8 miles to an intersection with Gold Camp Road. Go left on Gold Camp Road for 0.9 mile and park on the right, near a metal trail sign and a side road leading to the right. Regular cars can reach this point.

COMMENTS: This used to be a popular hike, with wooden stairs for the final ascent to the summit. Some of the wood from these steps can still be found near the top. The final part of this hike requires some caution, since the route gets obscure near the top. The rocky summit projection to the south is designated St. Peters Dome. This hike also involves the lovely and historic Old Stage Road, which connects Colorado Springs with Cripple Creek. An old railroad bed for transporting Cripple Creek gold at the turn of the last century, Theodore Roosevelt described the road as "…bankrupting the English language."

THE ROUTE: From the parking area, with its great view north to Colorado Springs, hike north-northwest, following the trail as it curves to the right and enters the trees. After 0.5 mile from the trailhead, go left (south) at a fork. (The right fork takes you up difficult terrain to the lower, north summit.) Follow this left fork around rocky cliffs before curving up and to the right for the final segment to the top. There is no trail for the final 50 yards.

Easily ascend the rocks to a flat, unmarked summit. Enjoy the view and retrace your ascent route back to the trailhead.

10 Cheesman Mountain 7,933 Feet

DISTANCE: 0.8 mile each way

STARTING ELEVATION: 7,180 feet

ELEVATION GAIN: 853 feet (includes 100 feet extra each way)

HIKING TIME: Up in 34 minutes, down in 26 minutes

TRAIL: None, all bushwhacking with some easy scrambling

SEASON: Late April to early November

MAPS: Trails Illustrated #105 & 135

NEAREST LANDMARK: Deckers

GETTING THERE: From US-285 at Pine Junction, drive south on Jefferson County Road 126 through Buffalo Creek for a total of 22.5 miles. Turn right onto a dirt road, passing up and west for 2.1 miles to a fork. (The right fork goes to Lost Valley Ranch in 7.0 miles, and the left goes to Cheesman Reservoir in 0.72 mile.)

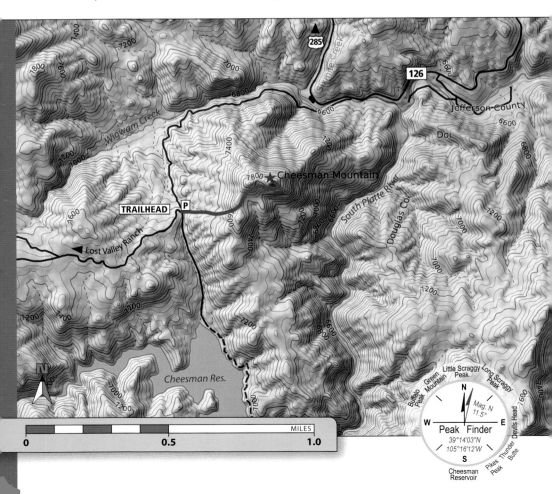

Park near this fork. Observe any posted parking directives due to the 2002 Hayman Fire.

COMMENTS: Named after Walter S. Cheesman, a Denver businessman from around the turn of the twentieth century, this peak can be reached even into November. The reservoir to the south also carries the same name and was formed by construction of the dam between 1900 and 1905.

On June 8, 2002, this area was engulfed by the largest wildfire in Colorado's history. The human-caused Hayman Fire charred over 135,000 acres, burned 133 residences, and took nearly six weeks and hundreds of firefighters to control. Cheesman

The summit boulder is only for skilled climbers.

Mountain was heavily burned over in places. Fifteen years later, the forest is on the road to recovery though evidence of the fire is still quite visible.

THE ROUTE: Hike up and east to a rather steep false summit and a ridge that leads to the top. Some easy use of hands may be needed in reaching this ridge. Once on the ridge, continue northeast, skirting another false summit on its south side, to the true summit—a huge boulder, unclimbable except with technical assistance. Some wires extend downward from its top, but these do not appear safe. Two USGS markers are present on the eastern edge of a rocky mesa, adjacent to the summit boulder. Return by your ascent route.

Looking down on Cheesman Reservoir

11 The Brother 7,810 Feet

DISTANCE: 0.7 mile on ascent, 1.5 miles on descent (loop)

STARTING ELEVATION: 7,480 feet

ELEVATION GAIN: 465 feet (includes 135 extra feet)

HIKING TIME: Up in 21 minutes, down in 38 minutes

TRAIL: All the way

SEASON: Early April to late November

MAPS: Trails Illustrated #100; Alderfer-Three Sisters Park Map

NEAREST LANDMARK: Evergreen

GETTING THERE: At the center of the town of Evergreen, from the intersection of CO-74 and Jefferson County Road 73, drive south-southwest for 0.6 mile on Jefferson County Road 73. Then turn right onto Buffalo Park Road and drive on this paved road for 1.3 miles. Park on the right at the trailhead parking area.

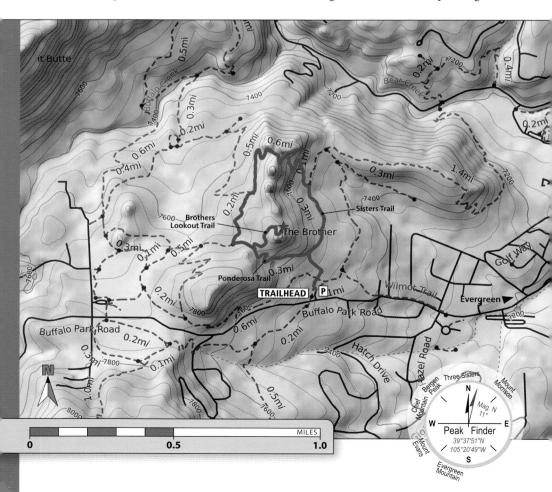

COMMENTS: Ever since Evergreen was settled, the four rock outcrops known as The Three Sisters and The Brother have been local landmarks. This hike is part of Alderfer-Three Sisters Park in the Jefferson County Open Space system. The 770-acre park boasts a mix of ponderosa pine forest, open meadows, and granite boulders. There is no park fee and the trails are well marked. Dogs must be kept on leash and motor vehicles are forbidden on the trails.

In the summer, hawks and turkey vultures can often be spotted from a perch on The Brother, riding up on thermals from the valley below.

THE ROUTE: Start up the trail, to the left of the signboard, traveling north-northwest. Within 50 yards, continue straight (north-northeast) at a four-way intersection on the Sisters Trail. After another 120 yards, turn left onto the Ponderosa Trail and begin your clockwise loop. Ascend 0.3 mile to a ridge and turn right onto the Brothers Lookout Trail, rising in 0.2 mile to the rocky summit and a benchmark. Enjoy the great views before returning to the last fork at the ridge.

To continue the loop, descend 75 yards to the right and take the right fork onto the Sisters Trail, circling back 1.0 mile to where your loop began. En route to this point, stay on the Sisters Trail and avoid the Hidden Fawn Trail. From the loop onset point, descend south for 0.2 mile back to the trailhead.

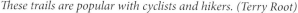
These trails are popular with cyclists and hikers. (Terry Root)

12 Lichen Peak 6,566 Feet

DISTANCE: 3.6 miles total loop

STARTING ELEVATION: 6,030 feet

ELEVATION GAIN: 596 feet (includes 60 extra feet)

HIKING TIME: Loop in 99 minutes

TRAIL: All the way

SEASON: Year-round

MAPS: Trails Illustrated #100; North Table Mountain Map (available at trailhead)

NEAREST LANDMARK: Golden

GETTING THERE: In north Golden, from the junction with the Golden Gate Road drive north on Colorado 93 for 0.7 miles and turn right into the North Table Mountain parking lot.

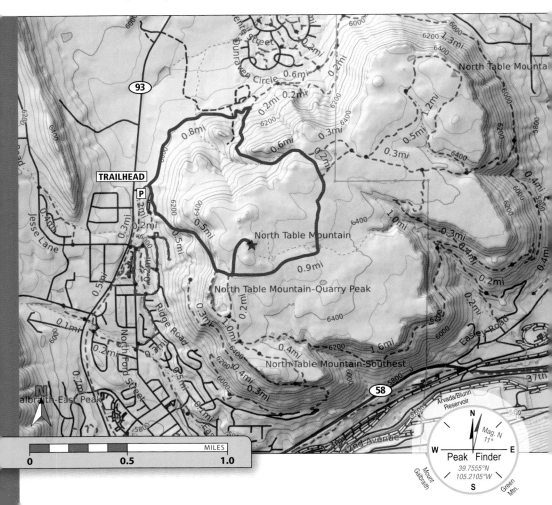

Lichen Peak is a small hump on the flat top of North Table Mountain.

COMMENTS: Lichen Peak is the highest point in North Table Mountain Park. There are volcanic, magnetic forces around the summit that will cause compass direction distortions. This trek can be done most of the year.

THE ROUTE: For a clockwise loop, begin north 0.8 mile to a fork. Ascend right on the Mesa Top Trail and follow it up to a junction with the Tilting Mesa Trail atop the mesa. Turn right on the Tilting Mesa Trail, which leads to the Lichen Peak Trail sign on the right. It is a 0.2-mile ascent from here to the unmarked summit. On your descent, continue right on the Tilting Mesa Trail, pass a quarry on the left, and descend steeply on the right fork back to the trailhead.

13 Fairburn Mountain 10,390 Feet

DISTANCE: 1.1 miles each way

STARTING ELEVATION: 9,310 feet

ELEVATION GAIN: 1,130 feet (includes 25 feet extra each way)

HIKING TIME: Up in 45 minutes, down in 35 minutes

TRAIL: None, bushwhack all the way

SEASON: Mid-May to mid-October

MAPS: Trails Illustrated #103

NEAREST LANDMARK: Black Hawk

GETTING THERE: This hike begins at the Cold Springs Campground, north of Black Hawk, off of CO-119 (the Peak-To-Peak Highway.) The campground entrance is 0.1 mile southwest of the intersection of CO-119 and CO-46, or 5.2 miles north of the intersection of CO-119 and CO-279 at Black Hawk. Drive

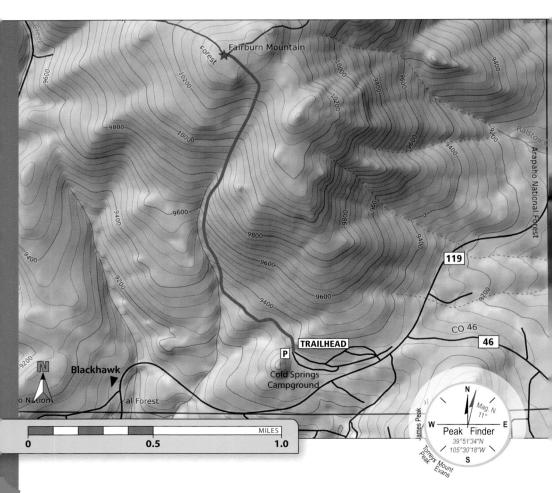

northwest into the campground for 0.8 mile and park near where a creek, flowing from the north, crosses beneath the campground's dirt road.

COMMENTS: This hike will provide good practice with map and compass, since there is no trail. Your route is due north but don't forget to factor in the declination—in this case, magnetic north is about 11.5 degrees east of true north. Try this one from May until October to avoid snow underfoot.

Fairburn Mountain lies just north of "the richest square mile on earth," as some early chroniclers dubbed Gregory Gulch. The colorful towns of Central City and Black Hawk in the gulch are experiencing a renaissance of sorts, since the beginning of limited stakes gambling in 1991. But with the newfound riches, you may notice on the drive to this trailhead that Black Hawk hardly resembles the historic mining and milling town that it once was. Vegas-like casinos and gambling tourists have largely taken the place of Victorian false-fronts and history buffs.

THE ROUTE: Proceed north, keeping the creek to your left. Quickly you reach a large clearing with excellent views to the south and southwest of the Mount Evans massif. Continue upward to the north and traverse a false summit en route to a small rock cairn at the tree-covered summit. The views are partial and to the west. Descend to the south, approximating your ascent route.

Fairburn Mountain from the southeast. (Eric Wiseman)

14 Devils Head 9,748 Feet

DISTANCE: 2 miles each way

STARTING ELEVATION: 8,780 feet

ELEVATION GAIN: 1,110 feet (includes 71 extra feet each way)

HIKING TIME: Up in 53 minutes, down in 48 minutes

TRAIL: All the way

SEASON: Early May to mid-November

MAPS: Trails Illustrated #135

NEAREST LANDMARK: Sedalia

GETTING THERE: From Sedalia on US-85 (south of Denver and northwest of Castle Rock), drive west on CO-67 for 9.8 miles and turn left (south) on Rampart Range Road (unpaved but well graded). After 8.8 miles at a sign, ascend the left road 0.6 mile and park near the trailhead. Keep right as a sign directs you to the starting point. (If the access road is blocked, then add 0.6 mile and 35 extra feet each way.)

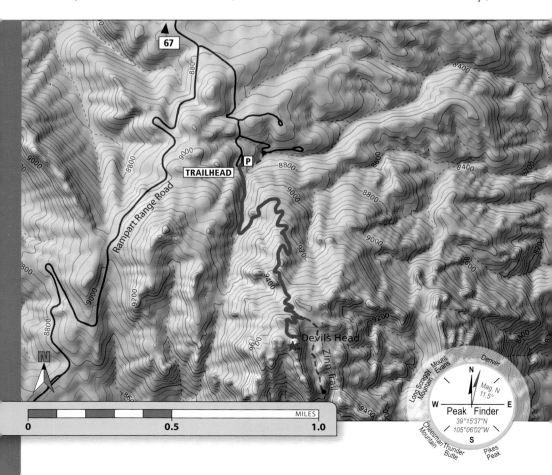

COMMENTS: This hike will usually be possible from May until November. Several informational signs and benches lie along this excellent trail.

Devils Head was originally called Platte Mountain until 1923. The devil's head is formed by rugged rock outcrops. The formation can readily be seen from Denver, prominent on the southwest skyline.

The tower and cabin at the top were built by the U.S. Forest Service in 1907 and replaced in 1951 by the Army Corps of Engineers. It is open to the public but certain restrictions apply. Please observe the posted signs. In particular, do not climb the stairs when lightning is present. Great boulder formations lie along this trail.

View from the summit of Devils Head.

THE ROUTE: Begin up to the south from the prominent trailhead. Pass through an area with many fallen trees on the left. Cross a wooden bridge and ascend steeply. A sign marks the halfway point. At a fork keep right, as the left trail leads to the Zinn Memorial Overlook of Pikes Peak. A plaque honors Commander Ralph Theodore Zinn, a graduate of the U.S. Naval Academy. Ascend to a narrow trail through boulders and descend to a cabin on the left and a clearing below the lookout on top of Devils Head. Read the warning signs before ascending 137 stairs to the lookout station and excellent 360-degree viewing. Be careful on the steps as you return on the ascent route.

15 Colorado Mines Peak 12,493 Feet

DISTANCE: 1.3 miles each way

STARTING ELEVATION: 11,315 feet (Berthoud Pass)

ELEVATION GAIN: 1,178 feet

HIKING TIME: Up in 55 minutes, down in 38 minutes

TRAIL: All the way on a dirt road

SEASON: Early June to early October

MAPS: Trails Illustrated #103

NEAREST LANDMARK: Empire

GETTING THERE: Drive on US-40 north from Empire, or drive south from Winter Park, to the top of Berthoud Pass. Park in the area on the east side of the pass.

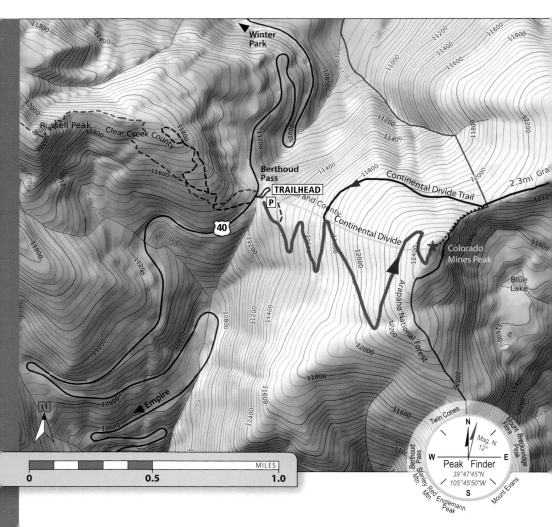

The commanding view makes this peak a good spot for communication towers.

COMMENTS: Berthoud Pass is named after Edward Louis Berthoud, who was born in Geneva, Switzerland. Berthoud was an explorer, a faculty member at the Colorado School of Mines and at one time, President of the Colorado Central Railroad.

Colorado Mines Peak lies astride the Continental Divide and on the boundary between Clear Creek and Grand Counties. It was named by Neal Harr, a student at the Colorado School of Mines, in 1954.

In 2002, the ski lifts began to come down on the historic Berthoud Pass Ski Area. One of the earliest established areas in Colorado, it was a favorite for generations but began to come upon hard times with the rise of much larger, corporate-run areas. If you hike this peak in June, you'll undoubtedly see a few diehards carrying their gear up the road to carve a few more turns before the slopes melt out.

THE ROUTE: Proceed southeast up a well-maintained road, beginning south of the lodge. Follow this service road, winding up through the ski area, to the top of Colorado Mines Peak. Several buildings are located on top, including a large telecommunications structure. Return to Berthoud Pass via the ascent route.

For extra credit, a ridge walk northeast along the Continental Divide will reach the top of Mount Flora in 1.3 miles. Mount Eva, after a false summit, is 2.0 miles more. Return to the saddle between Colorado Mines Peak and Mount Flora. The Continental Divide Trail descends west from there, contouring around the hill to rejoin the service road at about treeline.

16 South Peak 12,892 Feet

DISTANCE: 1.4 miles each way

STARTING ELEVATION: 11,921 feet (Weston Pass)

ELEVATION GAIN: 1,091 feet

HIKING TIME: Up in 60 minutes, down in 40 minutes

TRAIL: Initial 0.35 mile, easy tundra and talus walking beyond

SEASON: Early June to early October

MAPS: Trails Illustrated #110

NEAREST LANDMARK: Leadville

GETTING THERE: Drive to Weston Pass, connecting US-285 on the east with US-24 on the west: Either drive 16.2 miles west from US-285 (11.2 miles south of Fairplay) on Road 22 (the Weston Pass Road) or drive 11.1 miles east from US-24 (6.5 miles south of Leadville) on Road 7. Despite a few rough spots, this pass can be readily traversed in a regular car. Park at the pass.

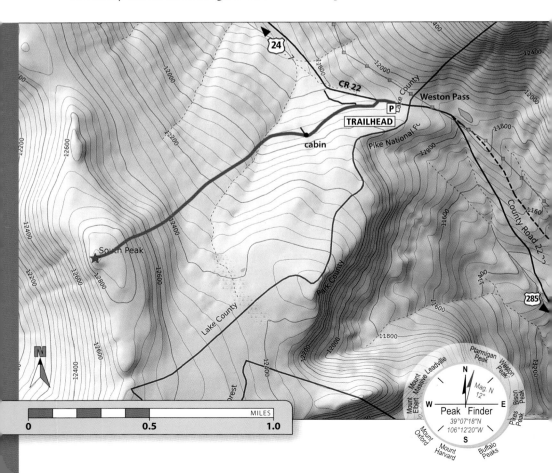

COMMENTS: Weston Pass was first an Indian trail and then a stage and wagon road connecting South Park with Leadville. On the east side of the pass lay the town of Weston, which once contained several restaurants and bars, serving traffic to the busy mining activities in California Gulch.

There is some confusion over who the town and pass were named after, as two prominent citizens named "Weston" settled in the area at about the same time. Phuo M. Weston arrived in South Park in 1861 and owned various properties along the old toll road. Algernon S. Weston showed up at about the same time and also acquired a ranch along the road.

As you travel the largely empty expanse of this road today, it's hard to imagine that in its heyday, the Weston Pass Toll Road was perhaps the busiest thoroughfare in Colorado. On September 4, 1879, 225 wagon teams were counted as they crossed the summit of the pass. Within two years though, the train route was completed to Leadville from Buena Vista and traffic dried up.

Beyond the miner's cabins is a tundra walk to the gentle summit.

THE ROUTE: Proceed about 200 yards west on the main Weston Pass road to an old mining road on your left that leads southwest. Follow the old road until it ends at some abandoned cabins. South Peak is visible directly ahead to the southwest, with white, rocky slopes leading to its summit. Cross the tundra and then some easy talus to a large rock cairn at the summit. There is a small radio tower nearby. Take the same route back to your car.

17 Royal Mountain 10,502 Feet

DISTANCE: 2.0 miles each way

STARTING ELEVATION: 9,095 feet

ELEVATION GAIN: 1,477 feet (includes 35 feet extra each way)

HIKING TIME: Up in 56 minutes, down in 38 minutes

TRAIL: All the way

SEASON: Early June to early October

MAPS: Trails Illustrated #108

NEAREST LANDMARK: Frisco

GETTING THERE: In Frisco, the trailhead lies on the south side of Main Street, 0.28 mile east of I-70 or 0.8 mile west of CO-9. A sign states "Vail Pass—Ten Mile Canyon—National Recreational Trail." Park near this sign.

COMMENTS: This peak, which forms the northern terminus of the Tenmile Range, features a fine overlook of Lake Dillon.

The trail to Royal Mountain passes through the ghost town of Masontown, which was settled in the 1860s by a group from the town of the same name in Pennsylvania. The founders apparently didn't know much about avalanches, because they built it in a prominent avalanche path. One hundred years later, artificial Lake Dillon was established.

The first part of this hike is on a popular, paved bike and foot path that extends from Vail, to Copper Mountain, to Frisco, and on to Breckenridge.

THE ROUTE: From the parking area, walk southeast and cross Tenmile Creek on a bridge. This is the only flowing water on this hike. Go left onto the paved bike path. After 0.3 mile, leave the path and enter the trees on a trail to your right, at a sign. Ascend south-south-east and soon pass through the remnants of Masontown. Follow the sign to Mount Royal and continue up and south by the right trail fork. The steep trail then reaches a fork after 1.7 miles from the trailhead. Go right (northwest) at this fork. (The other trail leads up Peak One.) After 200 yards, you reach an overlook of Tenmile Canyon and I-70. Go to the right at the rock pile and follow the ridge northward to reach the highpoint. The views from here are partially obstructed by trees. If you want a better overlook, continue down on a faint trail to the north-northeast for another 0.25 mile to a rocky knob. Be sure to return by your ascent route, since there are steep dropoffs to the east and north.

Looking out over Frisco and Lake Dillon.

18 Chief Mountain 11,709 Feet

DISTANCE: 1.5 miles each way

STARTING ELEVATION: 10,680 feet

ELEVATION GAIN: 1,129 feet (includes 50 feet extra each way)

HIKING TIME: Up in 45 minutes, down in 39 minutes

TRAIL: All the way

SEASON: Late May to late October

MAPS: Trails Illustrated #104

NEAREST LANDMARK: Idaho Springs

GETTING THERE: Drive south on CO-74 from Exit 252 of I-70. After 3.3 miles, turn west on CO-103 (the Squaw Pass Road) and go 12.4 miles (3.8 miles from Squaw Pass). There is a well-graded parking area off the road on the right (with ski lift machinery just below). Look for a wooden pole and a trail, going initially

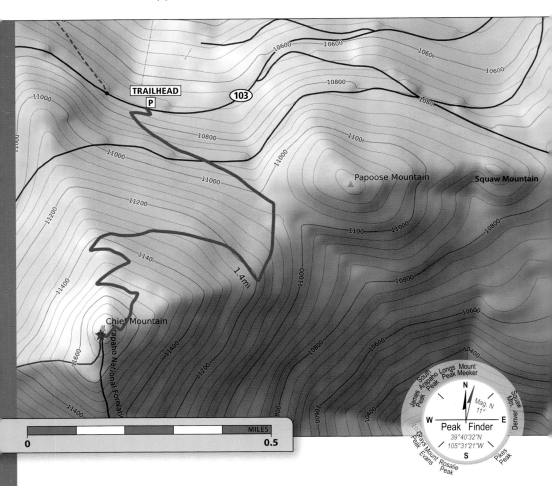

southeast, on the left (south) side of the road. Just above the trailhead on the south side of the road is a cement marker with "# 290" on it. Park in the clear area on the north side of the road.

COMMENTS: This readily accessible peak offers wonderful vistas of mountains and plains at, and near, the top. It forms a mountain family with Squaw Mountain and Papoose Mountain in the middle, despite regular letters to the Denver newspapers suggesting more politically correct names.

While Squaw Mountain bristles with man-made structures, Chief Mountain has more of a wild and natural feel to it. Closeness to Denver and a well-graded trail makes Chief Mountain a good choice to introduce out-of-town hiking guests to their first taste of the Colorado alpine.

THE ROUTE: Cross to the south side of the road and proceed southeast by trail. Enter the trees and cross a dirt road (the old Squaw Pass Road) after 0.4 mile. Continue up and southeast. After another 0.3 mile, the trail curves south at a cairn. (At this point, you are at a saddle with Papoose Mountain, an easy bushwhack up to the northeast.)

Continue on the good trail through a couple of switchbacks until past timberline. Then finally reach the rocky summit in a clockwise direction. A benchmark and a Colorado Mountain Club register cylinder lie at the high point. Enjoy the scenery, especially the fine views of nearby Mount Evans, and return by your ascent route.

The view of Chief Mountain from the east. (Terry Root)

19 Mount Zion 7,059 Feet
Colorow Hill 7,560 Feet

DISTANCE: Mount Zion: 0.6 mile each way | Lookout Mountain: 1.3 miles each way

STARTING ELEVATION: 6,900 feet (Windy Saddle) for each

ELEVATION GAIN: Mount Zion: 459 feet (inc. 150 ft. extra each way)

Lookout Mountain: 660 feet

HIKING TIME: Mount Zion: Up in 21 minutes, down in 18 minutes

Colorow Hill: Up in 38 minutes, down in 25 minutes

TRAIL: All the way to each summit

SEASON: Early April to Late November

MAPS: Trails Illustrated #100; Windy Saddle Park Map

NEAREST LANDMARK: Golden

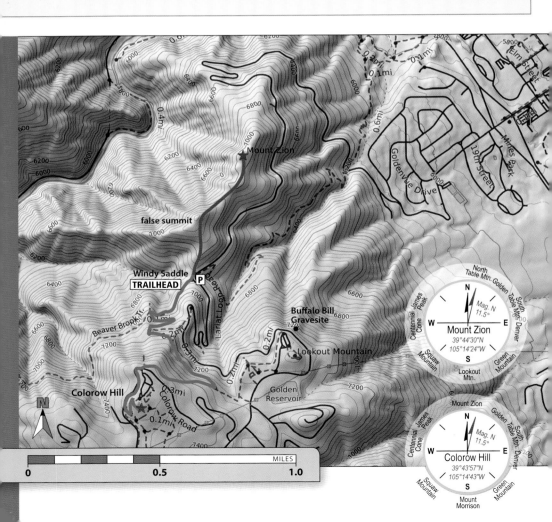

GETTING THERE: From the intersection of US-6 and CO-58 in Golden, drive 1.0 mile south on US-6 to 19th Street. Then ascend southwest as 19th Street becomes Lariat Loop Road for 3.5 miles to a parking area and sign for the Beaver Brook Trail. Park at the Windy Saddle.

COMMENTS: Mount Zion has a large letter "M" on its east flank, which can be seen for a considerable distance. Students from the Colorado School of Mines whitewash it each spring. Lookout Mountain, like Mount Zion, is one of several peaks so-named in Colorado. Its summit can be reached by driving up the Lariat Loop Road, beyond Windy Saddle. There are museums, restaurants, and homes around the summit mesa. The most interesting spot is the gravesite of frontier scout and showman, Buffalo Bill Cody. The panoramic view from Mount Zion takes in the entire Denver metropolitan area, an especially stunning sight at night.

Descending the Mount Zion Trail. (Terry Root)

THE ROUTE: For Mount Zion, proceed due north up the ridge on a rough dirt road from the parking area. A Jefferson County Open Space trail sign is present at the beginning. After 0.3 mile of steep going, you reach the high point of the ridge, but this is a false summit. Continue north on the ridge, losing about 150 feet, before you ascend an unmarked, rocky knob that is considered the summit. It will take you another 0.3 mile to get here from the high point. (You may wish to continue a few hundred yards farther north, and a bit lower on the ridge, to a metal pole in the rock, and the end of the faint trail.) Return via the same ridge to the trailhead.

A nice hike that can be combined with the Mount Zion ascent goes up Colorow Hill. From the parking area, take the Beaver Brook Trail west from the trail sign. After 0.3 mile, the Lookout Mountain Trail forks south, up through the trees. In 1.3 miles from the parking area, you reach the summit mesa. Just across the road is the Lookout Mountain Conference and Nature Center, which has exhibits and two loop trails. The center's building at 7,560 feet is the highpoint. A trail passes along the west side of the center and eventually connects with the Apex Trail. The Buffalo Bill Museum is another nearby mountaintop point of interest, on the east end of the mesa. To return, take the same trail on which you ascended.

20 Fitzpatrick Peak 13,112 Feet

DISTANCE: 1.35 miles each way

STARTING ELEVATION: 12,154 feet (Tincup Pass)

ELEVATION GAIN: 1,258 feet (includes 150 feet lost at beginning)

HIKING TIME: Up in 57 minutes, down in 40 minutes

TRAIL: To the saddle, talus and tundra beyond

SEASON: Early June to early October

MAPS: Trails Illustrated #129 and #130

NEAREST LANDMARK: Buena Vista

GETTING THERE: Drive to Tincup Pass: From the east, drive south for 5.7 miles from the US-24 and US-285 intersection (2.8 miles south of Buena Vista). Then turn west onto Chaffee County Road 162. Continue west on this road for a total of 16.2 miles to the historic town of Saint Elmo. Turn right in the center of town,

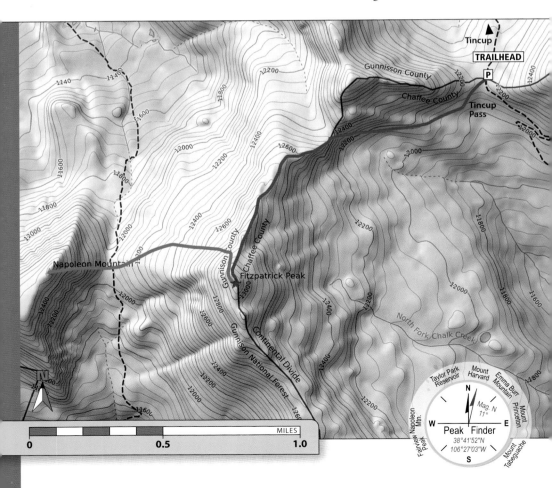

cross a bridge and turn immediately left onto Chaffee County Road 267. This road continues for 6.3 miles up to Tincup Pass. If the snow is gone, four-wheel drive and high clearance are needed to reach the pass.

From the west, Tincup Pass is reached via Cumberland Pass or Taylor Park to the town of Tincup. It is 6.7 miles east, and then south, from Tincup to Tincup Pass. Four-wheel drive is necessary for the final 3.0 miles to the pass from Mirror Lake. Park off the road near the sign at Tincup Pass. If your car is unable to reach the pass, add the extra distance to that given for the hike as described from Tincup Pass.

COMMENTS: Tincup Pass has been a route from the east to the town of Tincup since the 1800s. It was first a burro trail and later a toll road. Continuing improvements have made this road more passable in recent years. The road and pass are part of the Continental Divide Trail (Segment 26). Fine views of the Sawatch Range are yours on this hike from historic Tincup Pass.

THE ROUTE: Drop down about 150 feet to the southwest and keep to the left of the talus. Fitzpatrick Peak is the prominent mountain visible to the southwest. Find a sometimes-faint trail and head for the saddle to the right of the peak. En route you pass along a shelf leading to a large cairn at the saddle. The trail continues west and down to Napoleon Pass, but leave the trail at the saddle and go directly south up the ridge to a cairn at the top. The best route down is as you ascended. (For a side trip to Napoleon Mountain, descend the ridge, going north partway to the saddle. Then turn west and either continue west on the trail from the saddle or head more directly west to unmarked Napoleon Pass.)

Fitzpatrick Peak from Emma Burr Mountain.

21 Emma Burr Mountain 13,538 Feet

DISTANCE: 2.2 miles each way

STARTING ELEVATION: 12,154 feet (Tincup Pass)

ELEVATION GAIN: 1,384 feet

HIKING TIME: Up in 56 minutes, down in 34 minutes

TRAIL: Initial few hundred yards, tundra walk beyond

SEASON: Early June to early October

MAPS: Trails Illustrated #130

NEAREST LANDMARK: Buena Vista

GETTING THERE: Drive to Tincup Pass: From the east, drive south for 5.7 miles from the US-24 and US-285 intersection (2.8 miles south of Buena Vista). Then turn west onto Chaffee County Road 162. Continue west on this road for a total of 16.2 miles to the historic town of Saint Elmo. Turn right in the center of town,

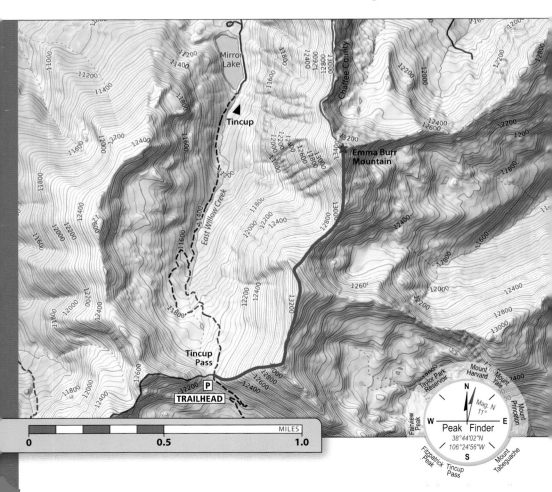

cross a bridge and turn immediately left onto Chaffee County Road 267. This road continues for 6.3 miles up to Tincup Pass. If the snow is gone, four-wheel drive and high clearance are needed to reach the pass.

From the west, Tincup Pass is reached via Cumberland Pass or Taylor Park to the town of Tincup. It is 6.7 miles east, and then south, from Tincup to Tincup Pass. Four-wheel drive is necessary for the final 3.0 miles to the pass from Mirror Lake. Park off the road, near the sign at Tincup Pass. If your car is unable to reach the pass, add the extra distance to that given for the hike as described from Tincup Pass.

The view from Tincup Pass showing the summit to the far left.

COMMENTS: No one seems to know how this mountain got its name. It is one of only about a dozen in Colorado that honor the fairer sex. It lies on the Continental Divide on the boundaries between Chaffee and Gunnison Counties and also between the San Isabel and the Gunnison National Forests. The hike is completely above timberline with constantly unfolding vistas and tundra flowers.

The town and pass both acquired their Tincup names because an early prospector reputedly carried his gold dust out in a cup.

THE ROUTE: Proceed on a blocked road, which leads up and east from the roadway at Tincup Pass. When this road ends after a few hundred yards, angle left (northeast) up over tundra to a saddle. At the saddle, hike north up the ridge, skirt left around a false summit, then drop briefly into another saddle. Continue north to a cairn on the grassy highpoint. Return as you ascended.

22 Green Mountain 6,855 Feet

DISTANCE: 2.25 miles each way

STARTING ELEVATION: 6,060 feet

ELEVATION GAIN: 895 feet (includes 50 feet extra each way)

HIKING TIME: Up in 60 minutes, down in 45 minutes

TRAIL: All the way

SEASON: Nearly year-round

MAPS: Trails Illustrated #100

NEAREST LANDMARK: Lakewood

GETTING THERE: The trailhead lies at a parking area on the north side of West Alameda Parkway, east of West Utah Avenue, in the city of Lakewood. This site is 1.75 miles southwest of Union Boulevard, coming from the east on West Alameda Parkway, or 0.8 mile east of West Jewell on West Alameda Parkway.

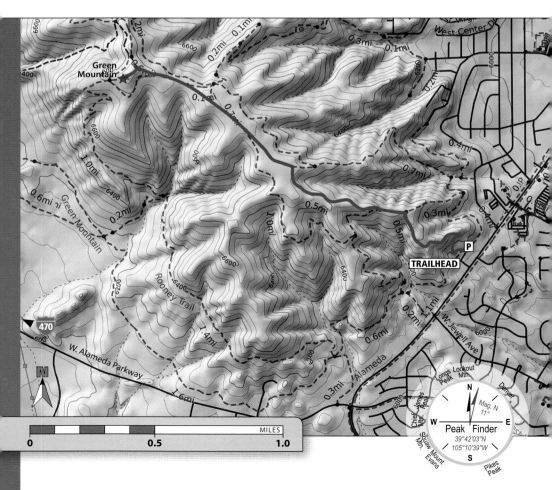

COMMENTS: This is the shorter of two Green Mountains in Jefferson County and the first named foothill as you leave Denver going west. Green Mountain is one of the excellent recreational areas of the City of Lakewood, a unique blend of the prairie and the Rocky Mountains in an urban setting. With 2,400 acres, the park is very popular with hikers, trail runners, mountain bikers, and equestrians. There is even a place for paragliding at the north end of the mesa.

While Green Mountain appears as a fairly non-descript, nearly treeless, rounded hill, it has some interesting geology. Green Mountain conglomerate—essentially a pile of gravel—makes up the mesa. This gravel was laid down as the adjacent Rockies rose and began to erode. Later, the valley to the west, which today contains C-470, eroded away to isolate the more resistant mesa from the foothills.

This hike can be enjoyed nearly year-round, except right after a snowstorm. The best time is perhaps late May, when prairie wildflowers and yucca bloom on the hillsides, and meadowlarks sing their liquid song from every mullein stalk.

THE ROUTE: Proceed north-northeast following the Green Mountain Trail as it curves gradually to the northwest, and then to the west. When you reach a radio tower in about 35 minutes, keep left and hike northwest on the summit mesa. Lose a little elevation. Near the highpoint, leave the trail and go left over grassland for about 50 yards to a large rock pile at the summit.

CMC
CLASSIC
HIKE

The trail to Green Mountain. (Linda Grey)

23 Lily Mountain 9,786 Feet

DISTANCE: 2.2 miles each way

STARTING ELEVATION: 8,780 feet

ELEVATION GAIN: 1,336 feet (includes 165 extra feet each way)

HIKING TIME: Up in 55 minutes, down in 53 minutes

TRAIL: All the way, plus a little handwork near the top

SEASON: Early May to early November

MAPS: Trails Illustrated #200

NEAREST LANDMARK: Estes Park

GETTING THERE: Either drive on CO-7 for 27.7 miles northwest from Lyons from the junction with US-36, or drive 6.0 miles south from Estes Park from the junction with US-36. A yellow call box and a trail sign lie off the west side of the road. Park close to this point, off of the road, and be careful due to the fast moving traffic.

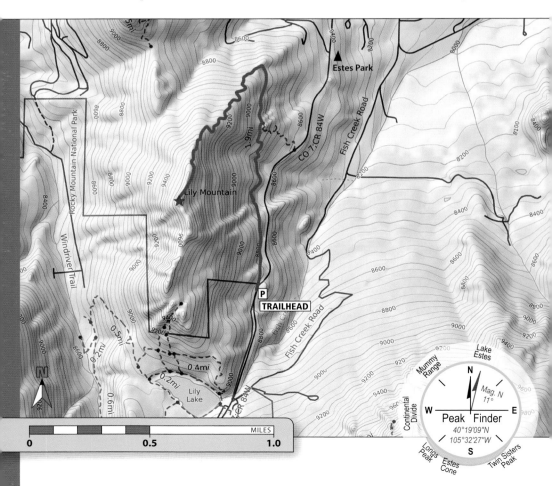

COMMENTS: This hike lies just outside of Rocky Mountain National Park. The vista from the summit is impressive, especially the view of Longs Peak. Lily Lake lies to the south and is not encountered on this route, nor is any running water. But this lake (located a couple of miles away on the highway) is a good after-hike place to stop and have a picnic. There is a Rocky Mountain National Park information center with restrooms and interpretive displays on the opposite side of the highway.

Lily Mountain is nearly completely covered with a thick forest of lodgepole pine. These pines typically are the result of a past wildfire, since they require heat for their cones to split open. Dense, mature forests of lodgepole, such as on Lily Mountain, are the least diverse of Colorado's forests, with rows of seemingly same-age, same-species trees that tend to exclude other plant species and limit the variety of species of animals.

THE ROUTE: Begin north from the trail sign. Pass a trail register and continue northwest for 1.1 miles until the trail curves up and to the left. Avoid faint side trails. Over the final 50 yards, ascend directly south-southwest at a faint fork. Follow cairns steeply to the flat, unmarked summit. Some easy handwork may be needed. If you reach a ridge saddle, you have gone too far. (In which case, the highpoint will lie to the northwest.)

Lily Mountain and Lily Lake. (Brent J. Murphy)

24 Douglas Mountain 9,550 Feet

DISTANCE: 2.2 miles each way

STARTING ELEVATION: 8,480 feet

ELEVATION GAIN: 1,370 feet (includes 300 extra feet)

HIKING TIME: Up in 75 minutes, down in 70 minutes (senior time)

TRAIL: All the way but often minimal

SEASON: June to October

MAPS: Trails Illustrated #103 and 104

NEAREST LANDMARK: Georgetown

GETTING THERE: From Interstate 70 at Georgetown, take Exit 228 and drive on the dirt road on the north side of the highway to the north for 1.3 miles and park at the road block. Regular cars can reach this trailhead.

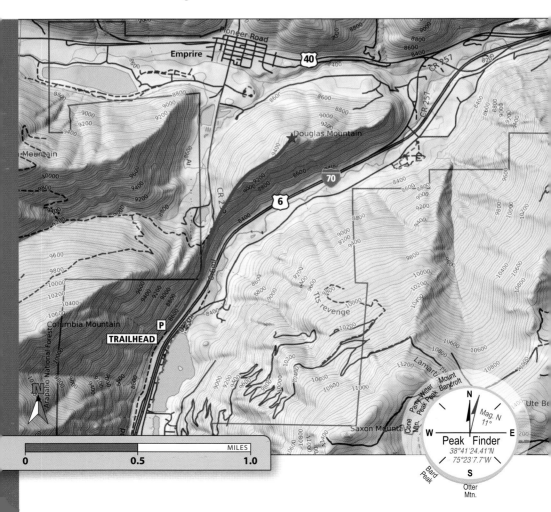

COMMENTS: The views from the trail down to Interstate 70 enrich this outing, which has some steep segments. Mountain sheep are often seen along the lower parts of the hike. Driving to Empire Pass from Empire makes this an easier hike.

THE ROUTE: Begin north on the clear trail that starts out flat and becomes a shelf trail up to Empire Pass and a road after 0.8 mile from the trailhead. (A road from Empire goes beyond this pass.) Continue north up a steep, rocky, modest trail that stays close to the ridge and weaves its way upward. Pass a false summit of boulders and continue north by trail to reach the flat summit with a benchmark underneath a four-pole teepee arrangement that is held in place by wires. Several peaks can be seen through the trees. Take the same trail to descend.

The view of Empire from Douglas Mountain.

25 Diamond Peaks 11,852 Feet

DISTANCE: 1.4 miles on ascent, 1.1 miles on descent

STARTING ELEVATION: 10,276 feet (Cameron Pass)

ELEVATION GAIN: 1,576 feet

HIKING TIME: Up in 66 minutes, down in 33 minutes

TRAIL: Initial first half until basin, open tundra walking beyond

SEASON: Early June to early October

MAPS: Trails Illustrated #112

NEAREST LANDMARK: Walden

GETTING THERE: Drive on CO-14 to Cameron Pass: From the east the pass is 59.3 miles from the edge of Fort Collins, at the point where US-287 and CO-14 intersect. From the west, Cameron Pass is about 33.5 miles east of Walden on CO-14. Park in the designated area by a picnic ground on the west side of the pass.

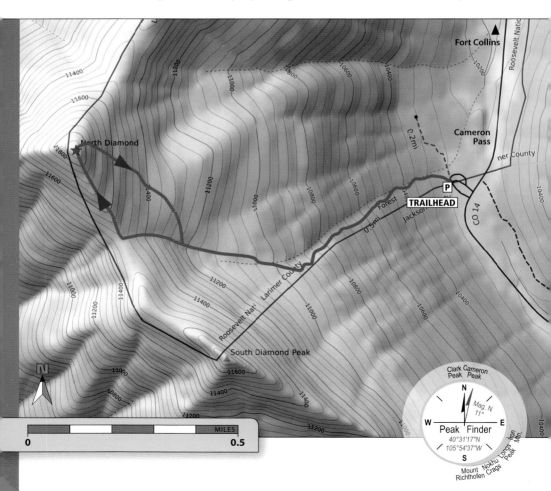

COMMENTS: This group of peaks is located about 30 miles south of the Wyoming state line. The details given describe the route to the highest of these peaks. They are to be distinguished from Diamond Peak, 8,668 feet high, which lies to the northeast, much closer to Wyoming, but also in Larimer County. Cameron Pass was discovered by General R.A. Cameron, who also founded the city of Fort Collins.

This northernmost portion of the Front Range is known both as the Rawah (an Indian word for "wilderness") Range and as the Medicine Bow Mountains. Structurally, they continue south of Cameron Pass and the highway but with another name change—the beautiful Never Summer Range, which is likewise a translation from an Arapaho name. The Rawahs are celebrated for summer wildflowers.

THE ROUTE: Head west-southwest from your car, up into the trees and find the trail. You will reach a creek, which you should keep on your right. Stay on the trail and ascend alongside the creek. The trail fades as you reach an open basin at the foot of the peaks. The highest peak will be visible to the northwest. Your target has a distinct hump near its summit. Proceed to the ridge on the south side of the summit and then ascend over tundra to the top, marked by a USGS marker, a cairn, a metal pole and several pieces of wood and wire. To descend, hike directly down (southeast) from the summit to the trail that you left in the basin.

The summit viewed from the south.

26 Mount Sniktau 13,234 Feet

DISTANCE: 2.4 miles each way

STARTING ELEVATION: 11,990 feet (Loveland Pass)

ELEVATION GAIN: 1,642 feet

HIKING TIME: Up in 90 minutes, down in 75 minutes

TRAIL: All the way

SEASON: Early June to early October

MAPS: Trails Illustrated #104

NEAREST LANDMARK: Dillon

GETTING THERE: Drive to Loveland Pass and park on the east side. The pass is on US-6 between I-70 (east of the Eisenhower-Johnson Tunnel) and the Arapaho Basin Ski Area to the west.

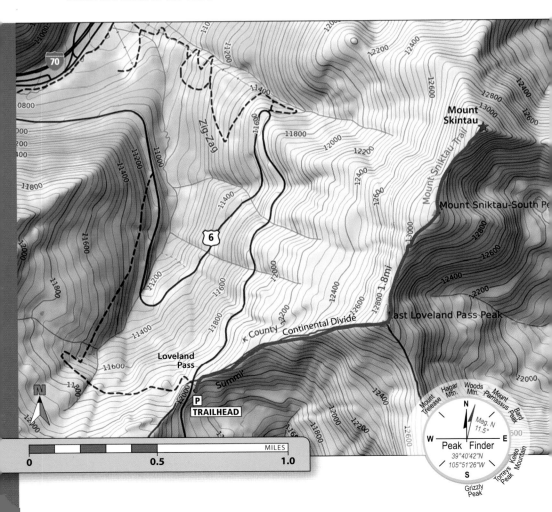

COMMENTS: Mount Sniktau can be prominently seen from I-70 as one drives west from Silver Plume toward Loveland Pass. While Loveland Pass is on the Continental Divide, Mount Sniktau is on a short spur extending north off the main crest. The pass is popular with late-season skiers and snowboarders looking for that last turn before the snow disappears. June hikers will likely share the trail with a few of them.

The easy access from the Front Range draws those who want to ascend a high peak from a very high trailhead. Sniktau was the nom de plume of E.H.N Patterson, a Clear Creek County journalist in the mid-1800s.

THE ROUTE: Take the clear trail going east and then northeast as it ascends steeply 1.0 mile to the ridge and passes a trail on the right after 0.5 mile from the trailhead. At the large cairn on the ridge, turn left and follow the trail up to a false summit at 13,152 feet. The trail then descends to a saddle before rising to the Mount Sniktau summit, a benchmark, and a cairn. The views from here are special—check them out before returning by your ascent route.

Mount Sniktau from Loveland Pass. (Eric Wiseman)

27 Glacier Peak 12,853 Feet

DISTANCE: 2.9 miles each way

STARTING ELEVATION: 11,585 feet (Georgia Pass)

ELEVATION GAIN: 1,668 feet (includes 200 feet extra each way)

HIKING TIME: Up in 77 minutes, down in 65 minutes

TRAIL: All the way until just below the summit

SEASON: Early June to early October

MAPS: Trails Illustrated #109

NEAREST LANDMARK: Jefferson

GETTING THERE: At the town of Jefferson in South Park, drive northwest from US-285 on the National Forest access road (marked "Michigan Creek Road"). Avoid the right fork at mile 2.0. Turn right at mile 2.9 onto Road 54. Keep to the main road, pass a fee station, reaching Georgia Pass at mile 11.9. Park off the

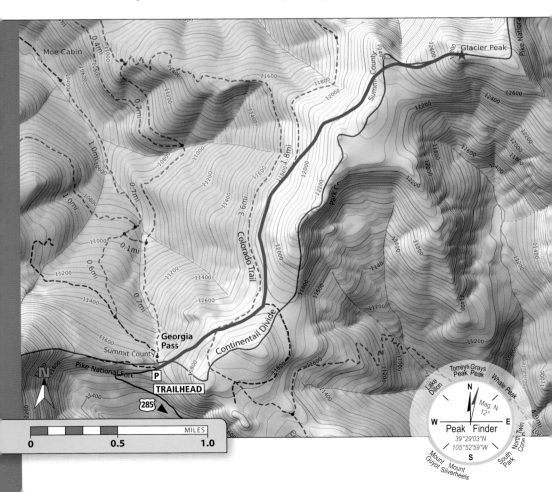

road. In most years, cars with good clearance can make it all the way to the pass, but sometimes visitors will be forced to stop and hike the final mile or so. If that is the case, then add an extra mile each way to the distance listed above. Access from the opposite end at CO-9, north of Breckenridge, is via a difficult four-wheel drive road.

Hiking the Continental Divide to Glacier Peak.

COMMENTS: The town of Jefferson was once a gold mining camp, and later, a railroad shipping station. The railroad tracks were removed in the 1930s. The town, Jefferson Lake, Jefferson Creek, and Jefferson Hill were all named to honor President Thomas Jefferson.

The route, entirely above treeline, mostly follows the Continental Divide Trail and provides lovely vistas. It also crosses Segment 6 of the 468-mile Colorado Trail, one of the most popular long-distance trails in the country. The CT winds its way through the heart of the Rockies between Denver and Durango, crossing eight mountain ranges en route. Segment 6, between Kenosha Pass and Breckenridge, is the longest at 32 miles.

THE ROUTE: Begin hiking up the old, rough road to the north. In less than 0.5 mile, cross the Colorado Trail and continue up the road to a four-way intersection. Continue north-northeast on the road, now closed to vehicles. Pass over two subpeaks on Glacier Ridge and reach a ridge at mile 2.8. Leave the road here and ascend right (east-southeast) over tundra for another 0.1 mile to a rock pile and USGS benchmark at the top of Glacier Peak. A subpeak lies to the east, as does Whale Peak, another 1.5 miles along the Divide. The easiest return from Glacier Peak descends directly south to the road and then back along the ascent route.

28 Geneva Mountain 12,335 Feet

DISTANCE: 3.5 miles each way

STARTING ELEVATION: 11,669 feet

ELEVATION GAIN: 1,636 feet (includes 485 feet extra each way)

HIKING TIME: Up in 88 minutes, down in 86 minutes

TRAIL: First half, tundra walking beyond

SEASON: Early June to early October

MAPS: Trails Illustrated #104

NEAREST LANDMARK: Georgetown

GETTING THERE: Drive to Guanella Pass, either heading north from the town of Grant at US-285 for 13.0 miles or south from Georgetown off of I-70 at Exit 238 for 10.0 miles. Park at the pass in the designated area by a information sign on the east side of the road. Regular cars can traverse Guanella Pass from either the north or south access route.

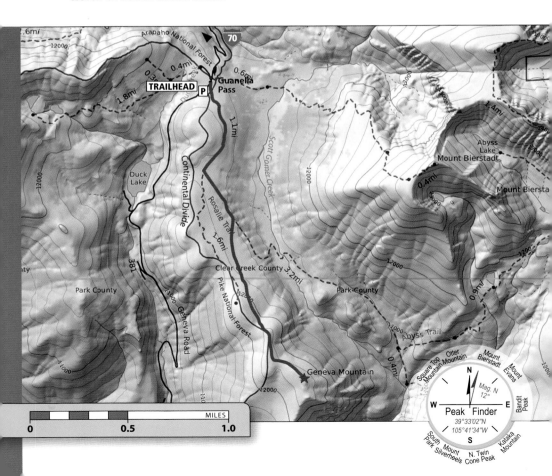

Geneva Mountain from Guanella Pass.

COMMENTS: This Geneva Mountain is not to be confused with Geneva Peak, north of Webster Pass and farther southwest in Park County. Guanella Pass was named after Byron Guanella, a Clear Creek County Commissioner who promoted work on the pass. The 23-mile road is a designated Scenic Byway and is now paved.

This hike is all above timberline and therefore affords extensive vistas over its entire length. You are likely to spot hikers scaling the nearby fourteener, Mount Bierstadt, as well as get a look at its rugged Sawtooth Ridge. You are advised to arrive early, as the parking lot for this popular area fills up quickly in the summer. The area is critical to wildlife also. The thick stands of willows in the bottomland between Geneva Mountain and Mount Bierstadt attract large numbers of ptarmigan in the winter, seeking food and shelter. Elk favor the area for dropping their calves in the spring.

WILD.
AREA

THE ROUTE: Begin hiking south-southeast on the trail from the Guanella Pass parking area. In 0.25 mile, take the left fork and continue on Trail #603. Within another 0.5 mile, you will see Geneva Mountain and two subpeaks to its right. Continue on an old road for another 0.75 mile from the trailhead, then leave the road and ascend southeast, mostly over tundra. Skirt the first subpeak to the left (east) and cross directly over the second subpeak to reach the top of Geneva Mountain, with its small rock pile and register jar.

29 Mount Volz 12,589 Feet

DISTANCE: 1.75 miles each way

STARTING ELEVATION: 10,900 feet

ELEVATION GAIN: 1,789 feet

HIKING TIME: Up in 79 minutes, down in 58 minutes

TRAIL: Initial 0.9 mile, tundra and talus beyond

SEASON: Early June to early October

MAPS: Trails Illustrated #109

NEAREST LANDMARK: Fairplay

GETTING THERE: From 10.0 miles north of Fairplay on US-285, drive north on Boreas Pass Road (Park County Road 33) through the town of Como, for a total of 8.2 miles. (A longer access from the north is by way of Breckenridge on Boreas Pass Road, 3.1 miles south of Boreas Pass.) At a bend in the road and a creek

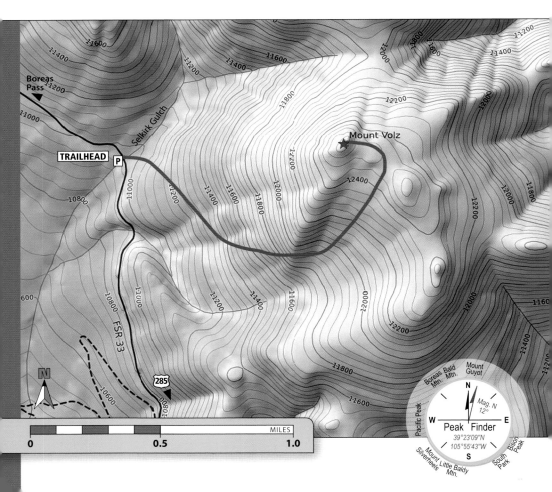

crossing, park off the road near a blocked-off side road that leads up and to the east. Regular cars can usually negotiate the entire 21.5-mile Boreas Pass Road.

COMMENTS: Access to this peak from the east is blocked by the Volz Ranch. To reach this summit, follow the directions carefully, since there are several unnamed high points in the area. Mount Volz can be seen from the trailhead to the east-northeast, and throughout the hike.

Named after the God of the North Wind, Boreas Pass was an important crossing between Breckenridge and South Park. The Denver South Park and Pacific Railroad operated a narrow gauge line along the present county road until the 1930s. After your hike, stop in Como to take a peek at the old round house, one of only a few still remaining from that period.

While this hike is pleasant at any time of the summer, it is especially fine in the fall, with gorgeous displays of aspen throughout South Park and along the pass road.

THE ROUTE: Hike east on the old road, soon curving south, then crossing the creek and rising to the east and timberline. As the road ends, continue due north over talus to a saddle, with Mount Volz to your left and a small rocky knob to your right. Proceed west up the talus ridge to a large summit cairn, a rock shelter and a USGS marker within a circle of rocks. Return as you ascended.

Mount Volz. (Terry Root)

30 Round Hill 11,243 Feet

DISTANCE: 3.2 miles each way

STARTING ELEVATION: 10,080 feet

ELEVATION GAIN: 1,163 feet

HIKING TIME: Up in 80 minutes, down in 70 minutes

TRAIL: All the way until 300 feet from the top

SEASON: Late May to late October

MAPS: Trails Illustrated #110

NEAREST LANDMARK: Fairplay

GETTING THERE: Drive south on US-285 from the intersection of CO-9 at Fairplay for 4.75 miles. Turn west onto Park County Road 5, which is the more northerly route to Weston Pass from the east. After 1.7 miles on this road, a side road leads to the right at a sign stating "Breakneck Pass—Private Property next 1.5 miles.

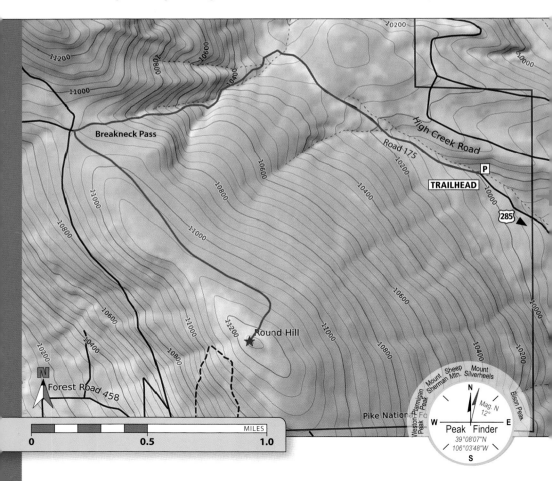

Stay on Main Road." Follow this road, passable to regular cars, for at least 1.65 miles to a sign stating that you are entering the Pike National Forest. Park off the road at this point.

COMMENTS: Despite the name, Breakneck Pass can easily be reached by four-wheel drive or mountain bike. Stands of aspen are common along the road, making this a good fall hike.

Settled in 1859, Fairplay was originally called South Park City and once had a population as high as 8,000. It was renamed as a retort to the gold strike at Tarryall, which locals called "Grab-all." After your hike, if interested in the history of the old west and western mining, visit the South Park City Museum in Fairplay—34 buildings have been moved here and restored and a narrow gauge train stands at the depot. It's all at the corner of 4th and Front Street.

Round Hill is visible on the right.

THE ROUTE: Proceed on the old mining road, designated #175, as it leads west, and then southwest, in 1.8 miles to Breakneck Pass. At the pass, which is well forested, take a mining road that leads southeast (left) off the main road. Follow this road as it gradually ascends to just east of the summit. Leave the road and hike about 100 yards west to the unmarked, tree-covered summit. Return by the same route. (About 50 yards west of Breakneck Pass there is a four-way intersection. Road 175 goes east and west, with the western road passing into Sheep Park. Road 426 goes north, dead-ending along Sheep Ridge, and south to join the Weston Pass Road.)

31 Kingston Peak 12,147 Feet

DISTANCE: 1.9 miles each way

STARTING ELEVATION: 10,470 feet

ELEVATION GAIN: 1,677 feet

HIKING TIME: Up in 82 minutes, down in 58 minutes

TRAIL: To St. Marys Lake, off-trail beyond the lake

SEASON: Early June to early October

MAPS: Trails Illustrated #103

NEAREST LANDMARK: Idaho Springs

GETTING THERE: Drive west of Idaho Springs on I-70 for about 2.0 miles and turn off at Exit #238. Go north on Fall River Road (which is designated Road 275) for 9.7 miles to a right-turning curve off the paved road. Turn left at this curve and drive north-northwest on a dirt road, with Silver Lake on your right (east) for 0.2 mile to a four-way intersection. Park off the road. Regular cars can come this far.

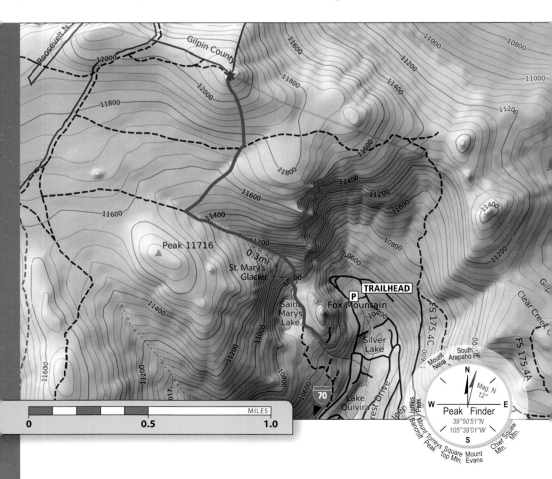

COMMENTS: Kingston Peak forms part of the boundary between the Roosevelt and Arapaho National Forests and between Gilpin and Clear Creek Counties. The best time for this hike is late August or early September when St. Marys Glacier is most easily traversed or bypassed. Kingston is also a popular evening hike in the summer, due to its easy access.

St. Marys Glacier isn't really a true "glacier," but rather a semi-permanent snowfield. Use care while on it, as several accidents per year typically occur here, including occasional injuries from uncontrolled slides into exposed rocks at the base.

THE ROUTE: From the four-way intersection, proceed south up an old mining road at the foot of Fox Mountain for 0.3 mile to a bend in the road toward the north. Follow a trail, which passes to the west from the road on the north side of the creek. In another few hundred yards, this trail will bring you to the east side of Saint Marys Lake. Continue on the trail past the north end of the lake to the area of Saint Marys Glacier, where the trail ends. Hike west and up, either around or through the icefield, for 0.75 mile. (The best route to avoid the snow and ice is to keep well to the right of the glacier.) At the top of the glacier, turn north and go another 0.6 mile over tundra to a summit cairn with two poles. Descend via your ascent route.

Looking up at St. Marys Glacier from the lake. (Terry Root)

32 Mount Epworth 11,843 Feet

DISTANCE: 3.25 miles each way

STARTING ELEVATION: 11,080 feet

ELEVATION GAIN: 1,263 feet (Includes 250 feet extra each way)

HIKING TIME: Up in 83 minutes, down in 72 minutes

TRAIL: Initial 3.0 miles, talus and tundra beyond

SEASON: Mid-June to mid-October

MAPS: Trails Illustrated #103

NEAREST LANDMARK: Winter Park

GETTING THERE: Either drive on US-40 for 11.8 miles north from Berthoud Pass or drive 1.75 miles south from Vasquez Road in Winter Park. Turn northwest onto Rollins Pass (Corona Pass) Road. Follow the road for a total of 11.0 miles to an abandoned railroad trestle on your left, at what is known as Riflesight Notch. Regular cars can make it this far, if there is no obstructing snow. Park here off the road.

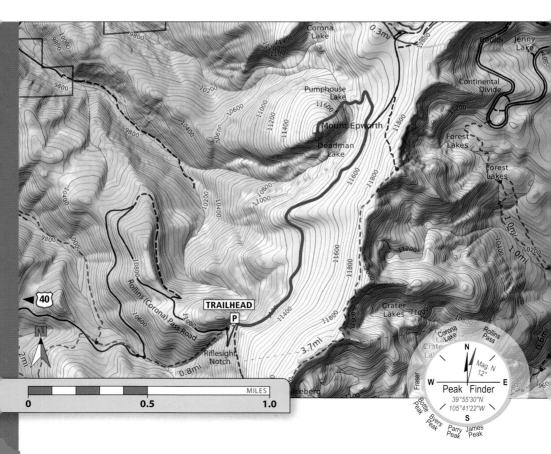

En route to this trailhead on the Corona Pass Road, keep right at 3.7 miles, continue straight (southeast) at a five-way intersection at mile 3.8, keep right on the main road at mile 4.55, keep southeast on the main road at a four-way intersection at mile 6.6, keep right at mile 8.6 and again at mile 8.85. In optimal conditions, regular vehicles may be able to reach Corona Pass and shorten this hike considerably.

COMMENTS: John Quincy Adams Rollins built a toll road over what once was called Boulder Pass, then Rollins Pass and later, Corona Pass. One of the highest operating railroads in the world also operated over this route from 1904 until the rails were torn up in 1937.

Epworth is the English village where John and Charles Wesley were born. The Epworth League, a national Methodist organization, named this mountain on July 8, 1905.

THE ROUTE: Continue on foot up the road, winding east and north for 2.5 miles to a point five minutes past a sign on your left with the number 17. Two lakes and Mount Epworth will be to the west (on your left). Near the level of the more northerly, Pumphouse Lake, an old mining road leaves the main road and descends to the north (left). After about four minutes on this road, take a left fork and soon leave this road, passing to the northwest of the lake and ascending the north ridge of Mount Epworth. Proceed upward and south, over tundra and talus, to a modest cairn at the summit. Descend by your ascent route, since the loop descent to the southwest from the top loses too much elevation and distance.

Mount Epworth with a view west towards Winter Park ski area. (Terry Root)

33 West White Pine Mountain 10,305 Feet

DISTANCE: 2.6 miles each way

STARTING ELEVATION: 8,288 feet

ELEVATION GAIN: 2,017 feet

HIKING TIME: Up in 76 minutes, down in 54 minutes

TRAIL: All the way on an old mining road

SEASON: Early May to late October

MAPS: Trails Illustrated #101

NEAREST LANDMARK: Masonville

GETTING THERE: Drive 6.7 miles west on US-34 from its intersection with US-287 in Loveland. Turn right (north) and continue 5.4 miles to Masonville, where the road continues as a "T." Take the left turn, and after 3.7 miles from Masonville, the road becomes unpaved. Drive 3.5 miles more to a fork. Take the left fork for

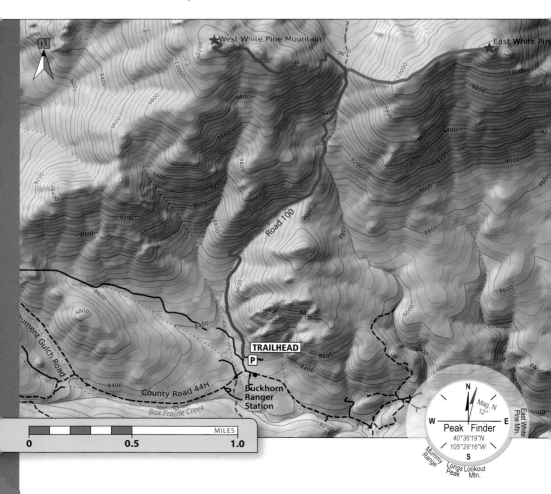

11.9 more miles along Buckhorn Creek to the Buckhorn Ranger Station on your left. (The total distance from the intersection with US-287 in Loveland to the Buckhorn Ranger Station is 31.2 miles.) Just past the Ranger Station, on your right, is Road 100 going north. When open, this road leads to the summit of West White Pine Mountain, but four-wheel drive is required. Park about 0.2 mile north of the Ranger Station, just off Road 100, near the site of the road barrier.

Another route to the trailhead is from Fort Collins via Rist Canyon to Stove Prairie. Drive south from Stove Prairie 3.8 miles and then make a sharp right turn at an intersection, proceeding 11.9 miles to the Buckhorn Ranger Station. Regular cars should be able to reach the trailhead by either route, from Loveland or Fort Collins.

COMMENTS: One of the best aspen hikes near Fort Collins, this area was heavily impacted by the High Park Fire in 2012. This hike provides an opportunity to experience the lovely Buckhorn Valley. Buckhorn Creek flows by Masonville into the Big Thompson River west of Loveland. Masonville was named after James R. Mason, who was born in Kentucky in 1849 and overcame great poverty to become a successful farmer and cattle rancher in the area.

THE ROUTE: Follow the road up and north, as it passes through many

A bull elk among the aspen along the trail. (Erick Wiseman)

aspen trees and a meadow. After 1.8 miles, you reach a saddle between West and East White Pine Mountains. A USGS marker lies just north of the road. Follow the road as it turns up and west from the saddle. In 0.8 mile from the saddle, the road brings you to the top of West White Pine Mountain, which is covered by ruins of an old lookout structure. Four cement pillars and a make-shift bench mark the summit. Trees block some of the views, but it is open to the southwest and west. Follow the road back to your car.

(If you want to reach the lower East White Pine summit as well, bush-whack up and east 0.7 mile from the saddle and 608 extra feet of elevation gain. The east summit lies amid some rock formations, which are easily negotiated. Do not descend southwest from the summit to save time, lest you pass south of a 9,130-foot subpeak and miss Road 100 completely.)

34 Tremont Mountain 10,388 Feet

DISTANCE: 1.0 mile each way

STARTING ELEVATION: 8,860 feet

ELEVATION GAIN: 1,528 feet

HIKING TIME: Up in 90 minutes, down in 60 minutes

TRAIL: Initial 0.25 mile, bushwhack beyond with some scrambling

SEASON: Early May to early November

MAPS: Trails Illustrated #100; Golden Gate Canyon State Park Map

NEAREST LANDMARK: Golden

GETTING THERE: Drive to Golden Gate Canyon State Park, northwest of Golden and northeast of Black Hawk. From CO-93, 1.0 mile north of Golden, turn west onto Golden Gate Canyon Road (Jefferson County Road 70). At mile 13.0, there is an intersection where Jefferson County Road 70 becomes CO-46. Continue

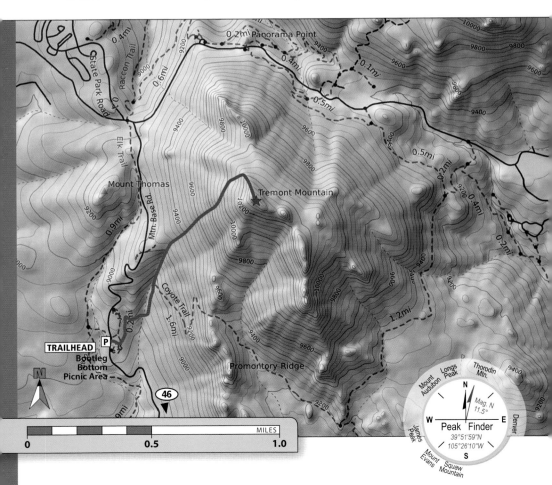

on to the park and pay the entrance fee. At a fork with the visitor center on the right, take the left fork and continue west on CO-46 for another 1.1 miles to the intersection with Mountain Base Road.

Alternately, you may go north on CO-119 for 5.3 miles from Blackhawk and then east on CO-46 for another 4.0 miles to reach Mountain Base Road. Proceed north on Mountain Base Road to the Coyote Trailhead at Bootleg Bottom. Park there on the right (east) side of the road.

Looking west from the summit at the Indian Peak Wilderness. (Terry Root)

COMMENTS: Tremont Mountain is the highest point in Golden Gate Canyon State Park. From the summit, you have a spectacular view west of an over 100-mile stretch of the Continental Divide.

This park is well maintained and contains nearly 60 miles of clearly marked hiking trails. After your hike, stop again at the visitor center, located just inside the southeast corner of the park, off Golden Gate Canyon Road. Here you will find displays and the Wilbur and Nellie Larkin Memorial Nature Trail. This trail is designed to be accessible to persons with disabilities and winds around the park's rainbow trout show pond.

THE ROUTE: Begin by going east, and up, on the Coyote Trail for about 0.25 mile to a sharp turn of the trail to the southeast, at about 9,000 feet. Leave the trail at this point and head northeast, up to the western (left) side of Tremont Mountain. The slope is quite steep near the top before you gain a ridge that leads southeast to the rocky summit. There is some easy handwork on this short, summit ridge. A hole drilled into the rock and an upright piece of wood are the only markers. The best route down is as you came up.

35 Mount Sheridan 13,748 Feet

DISTANCE: 1.25 miles each way

STARTING ELEVATION: 12,200 feet

ELEVATION GAIN: 1,548 feet

HIKING TIME: Up in 90 minutes, down in 60 minutes

TRAIL: Part of the way, plus off-trail tundra walking

SEASON: Early June to early October

MAPS: Trails Illustrated #110

NEAREST LANDMARK: Fairplay

GETTING THERE: From the junction of CO-9 and US-285 in Fairplay, drive south on US-285 for 1.25 miles. Then turn west (right) and follow Park County 18 (also known as Fourmile Creek Road) for 12.3 miles to two metal posts on each side of the road. (Keep right at the fork near the Leavick town site.) In most years, regular cars can drive to this point or close to it. Park here.

COMMENTS: This area is rich in mining history. The Last Chance Mine was located on the side of Mount Sheridan. Another large producer was the Hilltop Mine, located at the saddle between Mount Sheridan and Mount Sherman. Many of the miners lived in the nearby towns of Leavick and Horseshoe, which you pass in your car en route to the trailhead. The Denver and South Park Railroad once reached Leavick, whose population approximated 200 before the turn of the twentieth century.

While you may have the summit of Mount Sheridan to yourself, you will likely spot several hikers trudging up nearby Mount Sherman's south ridge. Many consider Sherman to be one of the easiest fourteeners because of its high start. Both Sheridan and Sherman were named for Civil War Union generals.

THE ROUTE: Proceed west up the road to the old Dauntless Mine. Then leave the road and hike up and southwest to the saddle between Peerless Mountain to the south and Mount Sheridan to the north. A faint trail goes up the ridge to a small cairn and a makeshift register atop Mount Sheridan. Descend as you came up by way of the abandoned Dauntless Mine.

For extra credit, you may wish to hike up Peerless Mountain to the south, adding 0.4 mile each way and 208 feet of elevation gain. Mount Sherman, a popular fourteener, is accessible via the ridge to the north.

Ascending to the saddle between Peerless and Sheridan in early summer. (Linda Grey)

36 Chalk Mountain 12,017 Feet

DISTANCE: 2.7 miles each way

STARTING ELEVATION: 10,600 feet

ELEVATION GAIN: 1,487 feet (includes 35 extra feet each way)

HIKING TIME: Up in 85 minutes, down in 60 minutes

TRAIL: All the way

SEASON: Late May to mid-October

MAPS: Trails Illustrated #109

NEAREST LANDMARK: Leadville

GETTING THERE: From Fremont Pass on CO-91 between Frisco and Leadville, drive south 2.9 miles and park on the right at a rough side road.

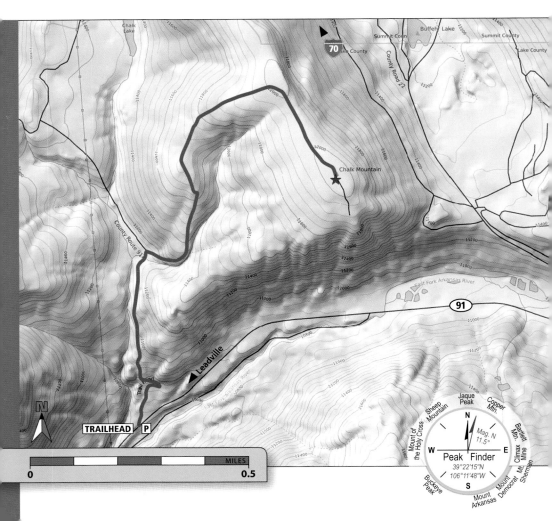

The Climax Mine has claimed much of Bartlett Mountain.

COMMENTS: Fremont Pass is named after the explorer, General John C. Fremont. The massive Climax Mine spills over hundreds of acres on the opposite side of the pass. During its heyday, it was the world's leading producer of molybdenum, which was used as a hardening agent in steel. In the 1880s, the strange, greasy metal puzzled miners searching for gold. But after its unique properties were discovered in the early 20th century, the property was developed into a huge complex that employed thousands, transformed the valley, and reduced much of Bartlett Mountain to mine tailings. The approach to Chalk Mountain from the east at Fremont Pass is now blocked by private property signs of the Climax Mine.

THE ROUTE: Begin north from CO-91 and quickly ascend on a steep, rocky road. With Chalk Creek on your left, the road reaches a fork after 1.0 mile. Go up to the right (east-southeast) on Road 134. At another fork, take either since they reconnect near the ridge. Then follow a clockwise arc to the summit and great views. Return as you ascended.

37 Revenue Mountain 12,889 Feet

DISTANCE: 1.9 miles each way

STARTING ELEVATION: 10,850 feet

ELEVATION GAIN: 2,039 feet

HIKING TIME: Up in 85 minutes, down in 70 minutes

TRAIL: Initial 1.0 mile, tundra and talus beyond

SEASON: Early June to early October

MAPS: Trails Illustrated #104

NEAREST LANDMARK: Dillon

GETTING THERE: Drive via I-70 and US-6 to the Keystone Ski Resort, which lies east of Lake Dillon. Turn south off US-6 onto Montezuma Road. Drive east up this road for 4.8 miles from US-6 to Peru Creek Road, which begins on the left at a curve in the road. Drive northeast up Peru Creek Road for 3.8 miles and turn

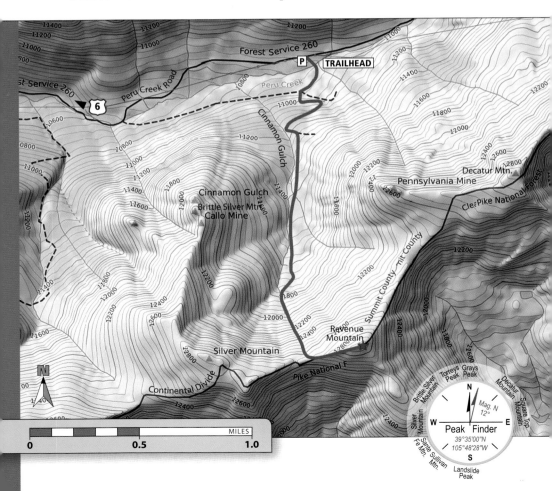

right off the main road onto an unmarked road. This is the road up Cinnamon Gulch. Park here, before Peru Creek is crossed. (With four-wheel drive, you can travel 0.85 mile up into the basin for a higher starting point. The hike information given is based on a start from Peru Creek.)

COMMENTS: Revenue Mountain lies on the boundary between Summit and Clear Creek Counties. Peru Gulch was the site of extensive mining in the late 1800s. This hike should be attempted late in the season when Peru Creek will be lower and more easily crossed. Easy ridge walking from this peak leads to other close-by summits for extra credit.

THE ROUTE: Head south, cross Peru Creek, and stay on the mining road, which rises into Cinnamon Gulch. Several side roads lead to old mining operations. At the first three forks go left, right and right as you head toward the basin. In a little less than 1.0 mile, you arrive at a large, open area and a road fork. Take the right fork and continue south as you ascend farther into the basin. Revenue Mountain will be visible to the southeast. Just below timberline, leave the road and go directly

Revenue Mountain framed by the door of a miner's cabin. (Eric Wiseman)

south over easy tundra to the saddle between Silver Mountain on the right and Revenue Mountain on the left. An old mining cabin sits below the Revenue Mountain summit. Follow the ridge, then go eastward to the top where there is a cairn and a small register jar. Decatur Mountain to the northeast, Silver Mountain to the west, and Brittle Silver Mountain to the northwest are all accessible by easy ridge walks from Revenue Mountain. Descend as you came up, unless you wish to walk the ridge to some of these other nearby peaks.

38 Mays Peak 8,283 Feet

DISTANCE: 3.4 miles on ascent, 2.8 miles on descent (loop)

STARTING ELEVATION: 7,120 feet

ELEVATION GAIN: 1,688 feet (includes 525 extra feet)

HIKING TIME: Up in 86 minutes, down in 59 minutes

TRAIL: All the way except the final 200 yards to the top

SEASON: Most of the year

MAPS: Trails Illustrated #137

NEAREST LANDMARK: Colorado Springs

GETTING THERE: From I-25 in Colorado Springs, drive west on US-24 for 1.5 miles and turn left on 21st Street and go 0.9 mile. Turn right onto Lower Gold Camp Road and stay on this for 5.1 miles. Park in the large area on the right as Gold Camp Road bends to the left. (This point is 7.5 miles from I-25.)

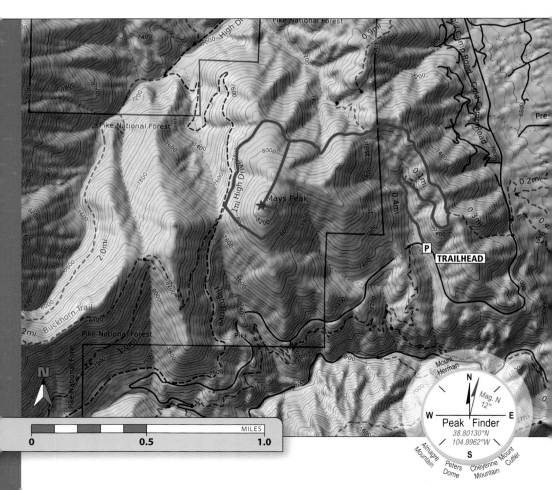

COMMENTS: The trails of North Cheyenne Canyon Park, southwest of Colorado Springs, are many. Due to lower elevations and location, they offer hiking opportunities for most of the year.

This trail to the top of Mays Peak is used by hikers, bicyclists, and motorized bikers as well. The gravel trail, designated as the Penrose Trail on certain maps, curves counterclockwise up the canyon and around Mays Peak to reach High Drive Road. From High Drive Road, it's a short climb to the top of Mays Peak and a good overlook of the mountainous landscape.

THE HIKE: From the parking area, begin on the trail (#665) up the canyon to the north-northwest. After 0.4 mile through the sparse trees, go right at a fork. (The left fork loops around to connect quickly with the main trail.) Soon cross a ridge with an overlook of Colorado Springs on the right. The gravel trail rises and falls as it curves left to join the High Drive Road after 2.7 miles from the trailhead. Trail 667 begins across the road. You, however, continue up a narrow trail to the east on the southern flank of Mays Peak. Follow this trail for 0.5 mile and leave it as it begins to descend. Bushwack steeply up to the west-northwest through a burn area a few hundred yards to the unmarked summit of Mays Peak. There are a few small trees at this high point but the views are still good.

To descend more quickly by making a loop back to the Penrose Trail, descend from the summit on the definite trail to the north-northeast and follow it 0.6 mile to a junction with your ascent trail. Then turn right (north-northeast) and retrace your steps back to Gold Camp Road. Be alert to fast-moving, wheeled traffic on the trail.

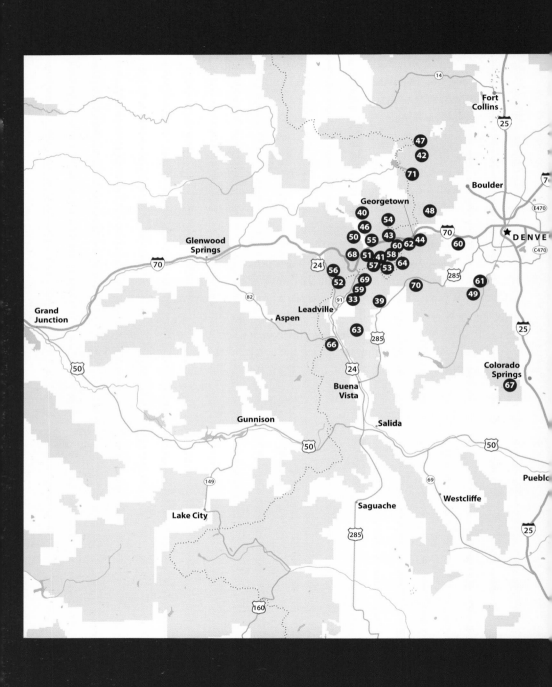

39 Little Baldy Mountain 12,142 Feet

DISTANCE: 2.0 miles each way

STARTING ELEVATION: 10,240 feet

ELEVATION GAIN: 2,002 feet (includes 50 feet extra each way)

HIKING TIME: Up in 88 minutes, down in 76 minutes

TRAIL: Initial 0.5 mile, bushwhacking beyond

SEASON: Early June to early October

MAPS: Trails Illustrated #109

NEAREST LANDMARK: Fairplay

GETTING THERE: From 10.0 miles north of Fairplay on US-285, drive north on Boreas Pass Road (Park County Road 33) through the town of Como for 3.4 miles and arrive at a fork. The right fork goes to Boreas Pass. Take the left fork, west and then northwest, for 0.8 mile, avoiding another right fork. Take a faint road

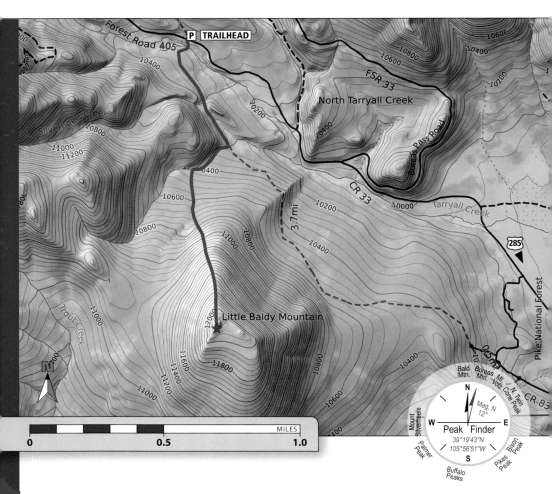

going off to the left (southwest) for 0.06 mile and park at a barrier blocking further vehicular traffic.

COMMENTS: This is the prominent peak at the southwest end of the Boreas Pass Road, easily seen from South Park. It is a favorite with the locals in Como, the little town that sits at the foot of the mountain. Como was originally the Stubbs Ranch and was named after Lake Como by the many Italian workers who lived there.

Some private homes exist in the area but no prohibitive signs are to be seen throughout this route.

THE ROUTE: Continue on the road, pass under the chain preventing vehicular access, and cross Tarryall Creek on an earthen bridge. Follow the road as it curves to the left (southeast). After 0.3 mile, take a right fork and continue southeast. The road soon ends at two private cabins. Avoiding any private property, hike due south and lose 50 feet of elevation as you descend toward South Tarryall Creek. Keep to the right of the creek and three abandoned cabins. Little Baldy Mountain may now be visible directly south. Enter the woods, following an abandoned road that heads west. When the road becomes obscure, continue to bushwhack up and south through the relatively sparse forest. You eventually reach a talus slope, followed by some more trees and then more talus. Above timberline, a cairn on top of a false summit marks the route. The high point lies at the south end of a mesa and is marked by a rock cairn with an embedded pole. Retrace your ascent route for the return.

Little Baldy Mountain and the town of Como. (Eric Wiseman)

40 Bottle Peak 11,584 Feet

DISTANCE: 3.1 miles each way

STARTING ELEVATION: 10,000 feet

ELEVATION GAIN: 1,704 feet (includes 60 feet extra each way)

HIKING TIME: Up in 95 minutes, down in 70 minutes

TRAIL: All the way

SEASON: June to mid-October

MAPS: Trails Illustrated #103

NEAREST LANDMARK: Fraser

GETTING THERE: From US-40 at the traffic light in Fraser, take Road 72 southwest. After 0.3 mile, turn right onto Fraser Parkway. After 0.8 mile on this road, go left on Road 73. Follow this road for 6.2 miles to a junction with King Creek Road on the left. Continue straight, parallel to Saint Louis Creek, for another

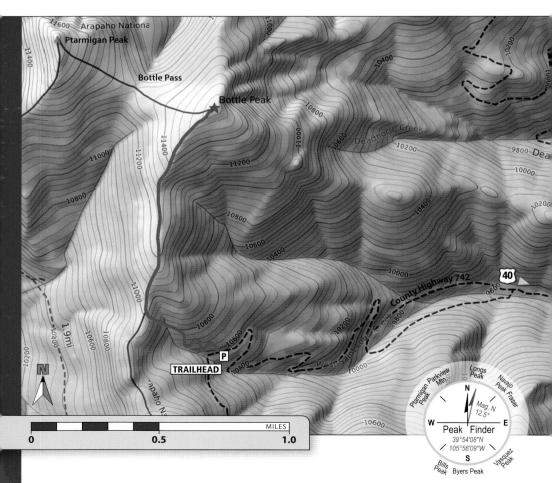

1.0 mile and take the right fork and go 2.2 more miles to another junction at a sign. Ascend the left fork another 1.0 mile and park off the road near the Byers Peak trailhead, where the ascent road is blocked.

Ptarmigan Peak (left) and Bottle Peak (right) straddle Bottle Pass viewed from the south.

COMMENTS: Grand County is named after its Grand Lake and the Grand River, the original name of the Colorado River. The town of Fraser, and the Fraser River running through it, were named for Reuben Frazier, an early settler of the area. The re-spelling occurred after a post office was begun in the town. Fraser calls itself "the icebox of the nation" due to the frequently recorded low temperatures there.

On the drive in, you will pass the headquarters for the Fraser Experimental Forest. They have been studying the effect of management practices here on water yield and quality since 1937.

THE ROUTE: Begin north up the blocked road for 1.3 miles to the Bottle Pass Trail on the right. Follow this trail west 0.8 mile to a ridge just below treeline. Then follow a series of cairns north-northwest to the top of Bottle Peak. (Bottle Pass is a few hundred yards west, with Ptarmigan Peak beyond.) Return as you ascended.

41 Kelso Mountain 13,164 Feet

DISTANCE: 2.75 miles on ascent, 1.5 miles on descent

STARTING ELEVATION: 11,230 feet

ELEVATION GAIN: 1,934 feet

HIKING TIME: Up in 93 minutes, down in 54 minutes

TRAIL: Initial 1.9 miles on ascent, final 1.0 mile on descent

SEASON: Early June to early October

MAPS: Trails Illustrated #104

NEAREST LANDMARK: Bakerville

GETTING THERE: Drive south on the Stevens Gulch Road from the Bakerville Exit (Exit # 221) of I-70 for 3.4 miles to the trailhead. The road is blocked just before the defunct Stevens Mine, farther south. En route to the parking area near the trailhead, take left forks at mile 1.35 and mile 2.3. A regular car can make it up this

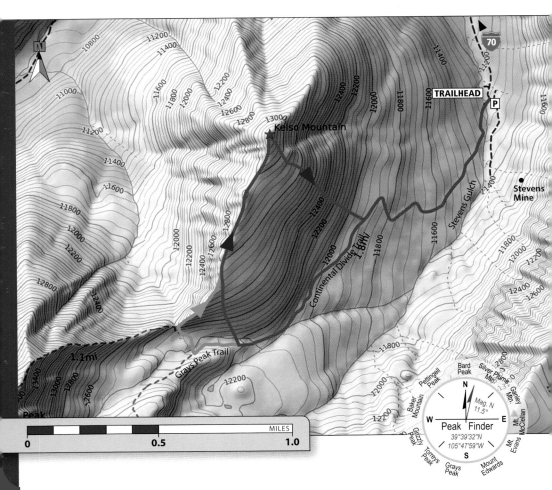

steep, rough road to the trailhead area. Restrooms and an information board are next to the large, gravel parking area. On summer weekends, the parking lot fills up very early with hikers intent on climbing the twin fourteeners, Grays and Torreys Peaks. Late arrivals may be forced to park alongside the access road.

North ridge of Kelso Mountain from Grays Peak Trail.

COMMENTS: This mountain is named after William Fletcher Kelso, a local prospector in the mining era. The mountain was to be pierced by a railroad tunnel that would pass beneath the Continental Divide to reach the rich mining regions on the western slope. But only a small portion of the tunnel was completed and the scheme ran out of funds when the rails reached Bakerville in the 1880s. A stunning view of the Grays and Torreys fourteeners can be enjoyed from the summit of Kelso Mountain.

THE ROUTE: Cross the pedestrian bridge over the creek and quickly access the old mining road going southwest up Stevens Gulch. This road is closed to vehicles. In almost 2.0 miles the road becomes a trail and crosses the creek amid two cairns. Leave the trail (which continues southwest up to Grays Peak) at this point and ascend north-northwest over steep tundra to gain Kelso's south ridge. Alternately, you may continue southwest on the Grays Peak Trail (a section of the Continental Divide Trail) for another 0.25 mile before heading directly for the Torreys/Kelso saddle. An old miner's cabin still stands here, just below the saddle.

Once on the ridge, continue north to the summit cairn. The best descent route is over the steep tundra to the east, to regain the trail that leads back to the trailhead. In early June, when snow still blankets this slope, bring your ice axe for an enjoyable glissade down to the trail.

42 Horsetooth Peak 10,344 Feet

DISTANCE: 3.1 miles each way

STARTING ELEVATION: 8,740 feet

ELEVATION GAIN: 1,902 feet (includes 148 extra feet each way)

HIKING TIME: Up in 110 minutes, down in 68 minutes

TRAIL: All the way to the base of the summit

SEASON: Early May to early November

MAPS: Trails Illustrated #200

NEAREST LANDMARK: Meeker Park

GETTING THERE: Either drive south on CO-7 for 12.0 miles from US-36 in Estes Park or go 22.3 miles north on CO-7 from the junction with US-36 in Lyons to Meeker Park. Opposite the Meeker Park Lodge is Colorado Road 113, going west past some cabins. This dirt road has a "Dead End" sign at its beginning. Follow this

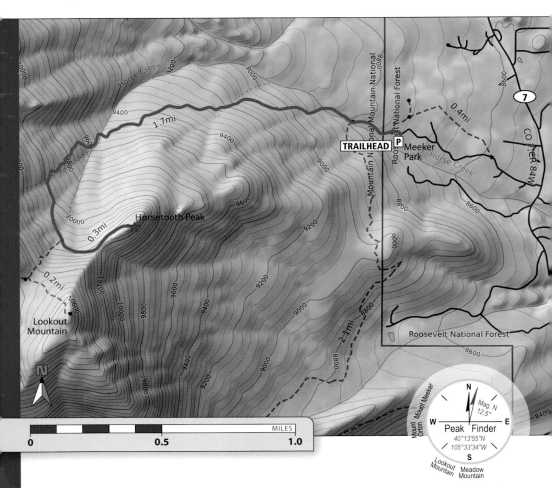

road west, a total of 0.7 mile, to where it ends near a cabin. En route, avoid side roads to cabins and stay on the well-maintained main road. Park off the road.

COMMENTS: Horsetooth Peak is named for the configuration of its summit. The distinctive summit boulder may prove unnegotiable for the solo hiker. A second person can provide the necessary support. No entrance fee is required to access Rocky Mountain National Park by this route. This is in a remote part of the park, most often used by mountaineers intent on climbing Mount Meeker's east ridge.

The distinctive outcrop on the summit gives Horsetooth Peak its name.

Pope John Paul II stayed at nearby Camp St. Malo on his visit to Colorado in 1993 and hiked on a portion of this trail. After your hike, you might want to drive north for 1.0 mile on CO-7 for a look at the dramatic statue of Christ erected on the site after founder Msgr. Joseph J. Bosetti saw a fiery meteor fall from the sky in 1916.

THE ROUTE: Unmarked trails pass east and west from where you have parked at road end. Take the trail west and in a minute you will enter Rocky Mountain National Park at a sign. Quickly pass a side trail on the left that crosses Horse Creek and leads to Wild Basin. The rocky trail rises as it curves gradually left. After 2.3 miles, pass a side trail on the left marked by cairns. Continue up the main trail to a saddle with Lookout Mountain above on the right. Turn left and follow a series of cairns leading to the base of Horsetooth Peak's summit boulder. Ascending the summit outcrop requires some climbing skills; be careful if you attempt it. Enjoy the views and return as you ascended.

43 Woods Mountain 12,940 Feet

DISTANCE: 2.3 miles each way

STARTING ELEVATION: 10,700 feet

ELEVATION GAIN: 2,340 feet (includes 100 extra feet)

HIKING TIME: Up in 90 minutes, down in 70 minutes

TRAIL: Initial 1.5 miles, tundra walking beyond

SEASON: Late June to October

MAPS: Trails Illustrated #104

NEAREST LANDMARK: Empire

GETTING THERE: Drive west from US-40 on the Henderson Mine cutoff road, 5.9 miles south of Berthoud Pass or 7.4 miles west of Empire. Pass the Big Bend picnic area and after 0.4 mile ascend left on Woods Creek Road. Continue for 2.9 miles to the parking area and a roadblock.

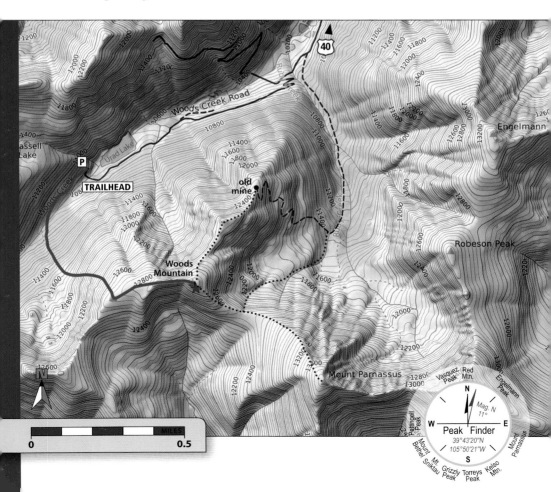

Woods Mountain and Mount Parnassus.

COMMENTS: From Woods Mountain, one can ascend the ridge to the east-southeast and easily reach Mount Parnassus and Bard Peak. If you do so, then the easiest descent is to return to the saddle between Woods Mountain and Mount Parnassus. Descend northeast from here to Ruby Creek. Pick up the jeep trail where it crosses Ruby Creek at just below timberline. Follow this jeep trail north, along the east bank of the creek, down to the intersection with the access road. Turn left here and walk west back up the road to your car in a little more than 1.0 mile.

THE ROUTE: Follow the blocked road 0.2 mile to a four-way junction with Urad Lake and a dam on the right. Continue straight above the lake on the road— the road will curve right and then curve left (south). After 0.5 mile from the curve south, take a right fork and keep the creek on your left. After 0.6 mile farther, cross the creek on the road, which ends just below treeline. Continue south toward the head of the valley and then go left up to a ridge going east—a faint trail may appear. Cross a false summit to the flat high point.

To return, either retrace your route or descend north-northwest over steep tundra to the Woods Creek Road.

44 Griffith Mountain 11,558 Feet

DISTANCE: 2.5 miles each way

STARTING ELEVATION: 9,100 feet

ELEVATION GAIN: 2,568 feet (includes 50 feet extra each way)

HIKING TIME: Up in 100 minutes, down in 60 minutes

TRAIL: Initial 1.25 miles, bushwhack beyond

SEASON: Late May to late October

MAPS: Trails Illustrated #104

NEAREST LANDMARK: Idaho Springs

GETTING THERE: From Exit #240 of I-70 at the town of Idaho Springs, drive southwest on CO-103 for 6.7 miles. At a sharp bend in the road, a dirt road leads southwest up West Chicago Creek. Drive up this road for 1.1 miles to an area on the right (north), just before a group of houses and a creek flowing under the road to the southeast. Being careful to avoid private property, park off the road in this general area.

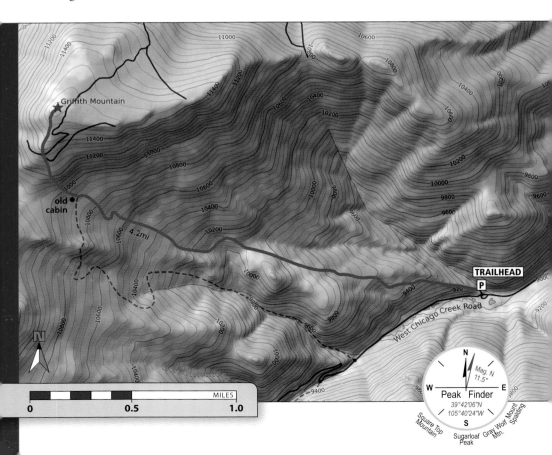

COMMENTS: This mountain is named after two early Clear Creek miners, the Griffith brothers, David and George. Georgetown was named after the latter. There are several mines on the mountain, mostly on the Georgetown side. As opposed to gold mining in nearby Idaho Springs and Central City, the mines around Georgetown were among the first in the state to pursue silver ore.

This hike passes by a large aspen forest carpeting the south slope of the peak and involves one mile of bushwhacking to and from the top. The views from the summit are best to the south, southeast, and southwest, with many trees obscuring vistas in the other directions.

THE ROUTE: Continue on foot up the public road, about 200 yards southwest of the creek crossing. Just past some houses on your right, leave the road and ascend steeply northwest. Within 100 feet, gain an abandoned mining road passing to the west. Take this road, continuing your ascent to the west. Stay on the road, which crosses a ridge and descends a bit, before resuming its upward, west-northwest direction. Eventually an old cabin is reached in a clearing to the left of the road. Leave the road at this point and enter a relatively sparse area of forest on your right, ascending northwest over many decaying tree fragments, all the way to the top. The summit lies on a small natural rock formation and has no identifying markers. Return by the same route, bushwhacking south-east about 1.0 mile until you reach the trail.

The aspen forests on Griffith Mountain make this an exceptional fall hike. (Eric Wiseman)

45 Mount Democrat 14,148 Feet

DISTANCE: 2.2 miles each way

STARTING ELEVATION: 12,010 feet

ELEVATION GAIN: 2,162 feet (includes 12 extra feet each way)

HIKING TIME: Up in 92 minutes, down in 67 minutes

TRAIL: All the way

SEASON: July to October

MAPS: Trails Illustrated#109

NEAREST LANDMARK: Alma

GETTING THERE: Drive on CO-9 5.6 miles south from Hoosier Pass or 6.0 miles north from US-285 at Fairplay to the town of Alma. Turn west opposite the post office and a gas station and follow the dirt road northwest along Buckskin Creek

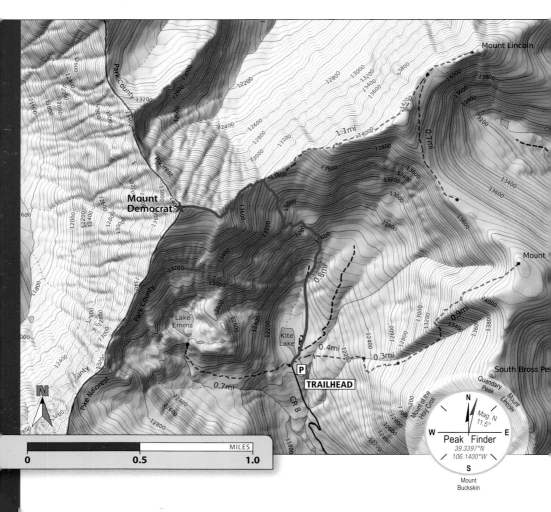

for 5.6 miles to a flat parking area just south of Kite Lake ; a fee is required. This road is especially rough for the last 0.7 mile and many hikers park before this final segment. En route on the dirt road to Kite Lake, keep right at mile 2.8 and left at mile 3.1.

COMMENTS: Of all the Colorado fourteeners, Mount Democrat may be the easiest to climb. The route from Kite Lake is very popular and can lead to other nearby fourteeners—Mount Lincoln, Mount Bross, and Mount Cameron.

The view from the summit of Mount Democrat towards Lincoln and Cameron.

THE ROUTE: Begin on the road to the north-northeast across the outflow from Kite Lake. Then choose one of two trails, which will reconnect and lead northwest to a saddle and an old mine shaft. Stay on the main trail. Ascend left (south-southwest) as the trail becomes more rocky. Cross a subpeak and pass cabin remnants and reach a cairn and register at the top of Mount Democrat. Unless you want to reach another fourteener from the saddle that you passed on the ascent route, return by the same trail that you took from Kite Lake.

46 Vasquez Peak 12,947 Feet

DISTANCE: 3.8 miles each way

STARTING ELEVATION: 10,280 feet

ELEVATION GAIN: 2,767 feet

HIKING TIME: Up in 110 minutes, down in 90 minutes

TRAIL: Initial 3.2 miles

SEASON: Late May to early October

MAPS: Trails Illustrated #103

NEAREST LANDMARK: Empire

GETTING THERE: Drive west on US-40 from its junction with I-70 for 9.6 miles, passing through the town of Empire. Turn left (west) at the big bend in the road, 5.9 miles south of Berthoud Pass. Continue west on this paved road, bypassing a left fork at 0.4 mile, for a total of 1.75 miles to the Henderson Mine entrance,

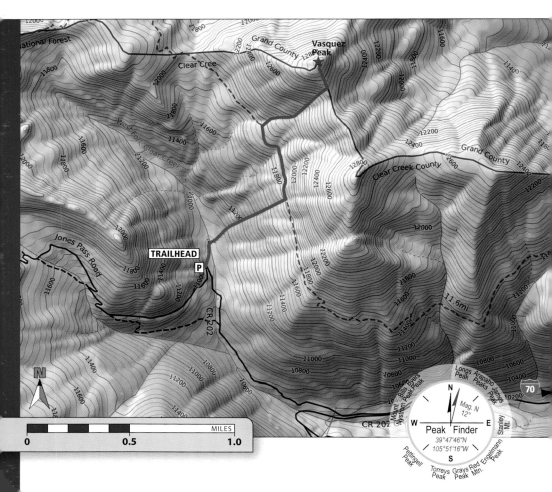

where a dirt road goes off to the right, ascending to Jones Pass. Drive northwest up this road for 1.45 miles to some old ruins on the right, just before the road crosses the creek. Park off the road to the right. Many regular cars can drive this far. (Note that sometimes this road is closed to vehicles at a point 0.5 mile from the mine turnoff, lengthening your hike).

Snack break near the summit of Vasquez Peak. (Lloyd McClendon)

COMMENTS: This mountain is named after Louis Vasquez, one of the earliest settlers of Colorado. Vasquez was a hunter, explorer, and fur trader. It is believed that he built the first cabin in Clear Creek County.

Vasquez Peak lies astride the Continental Divide. With its open, south-facing slopes, it is known as a fine, early season hike. The Continental Divide Trail crosses your route to the summit.

THE ROUTE: Begin northeast on the clear trail which ascends 1.2 miles to a junction with the Continental Divide Trail. Go left for 2.0 miles. Leave the trail and head northeast up to the saddle, then proceed to the summit. Return as you ascended.

WILD.
AREA

CMC
CLASSIC
HIKE

47 Estes Cone 11,006 Feet

DISTANCE: 3.0 miles each way

STARTING ELEVATION: 9,400 feet

ELEVATION GAIN: 2,206 feet (includes 300 feet extra each way)

HIKING TIME: Up in 87 minutes, down in 80 minutes

TRAIL: All the way, with easy scrambling to the top

SEASON: Early May to early November

MAPS: Trails Illustrated #200; Rocky Mountain National Park Map

NEAREST LANDMARK: Estes Park

GETTING THERE: Drive north from Lyons on CO-7 from its junction with US-36 for 25.1 miles or go south from Estes Park on CO-7 from its junction with US-36 for 9.2 miles. Turn west at the sign to Longs Peak Campground and drive for 1.1 miles to the parking area at road end at the Longs Peak Ranger Station

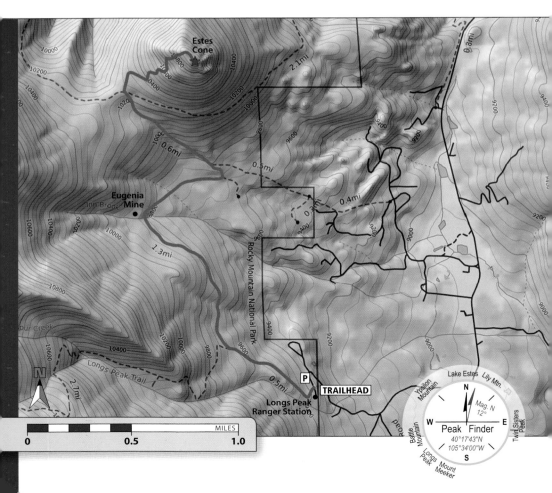

and trailhead. This parking lot fills to overflowing on summer weekends by mid-morning with climbers intent on scaling Longs Peak. Either do this hike mid-week or plan on an early start.

COMMENTS: This peak is prominent from CO-7 in the Longs Peak area. This perfectly formed cone offers 360-degree panoramic views of Rocky Mountain National Park. It is named after Joel Estes, who is said to have been the first settler in what is now called Estes Park. No admission fee is required for entering Rocky Mountain National Park at this trailhead.

The abandoned Eugenia Mine, with its spoil heap and rusty boiler, was not a success. Lack of valuable mineralization throughout most of the park prevented wide scale mining.

THE ROUTE: Begin south on the excellent trail from the Longs Peak Ranger Station. Pass a trail register and follow the trail northwest through the trees to a fork 0.5 mile from the trailhead. Go to the right and pass the ruins of the Eugenia Mine in 0.9 more miles. Continue north on the trail and descend into Moore Park. (A corral and fork are reached 0.6 mile from the Eugenia Mine.) Ascend the left fork to the north-northwest and, after a somewhat steeper 0.6 mile, reach a rock pile at a final fork. Take the right fork to the north, following a fainter trail and a series of cairns as the going becomes steeper. At the rocky summit block, follow the trail and cairns through a notch. Then descend briefly, before the final ascent to a large rock pile on top of Estes Cone. Some easy handwork may be needed. Enjoy the fantastic 360-degree panorama, especially west to Mount Meeker and Longs Peak. Be careful to retrace your ascent route, following the cairns back down to the rock pile and taking the left fork.

CMC
CLASSIC
HIKE

Estes Cone and Lily Lake with Longs Peak and Mount Meeker behind. (Brent J. Murphy)

48 Caribou Peak 12,310 Feet

DISTANCE: 3.9 miles each way

STARTING ELEVATION: 9,960 feet

ELEVATION GAIN: 2,640 feet (includes 145 feet extra each way)

HIKING TIME: Up in 115 minutes, down in 85 minutes

TRAIL: To within 100 feet of the top

SEASON: Early June to early October

MAPS: Trails Illustrated #102

NEAREST LANDMARK: Nederland

GETTING THERE: From the traffic circle in Nederland at the junction with CO-119, drive north on CO-72 for 7.0 miles and turn left onto Road 116 to the Rainbow Lakes Campground. Follow this dirt road for 0.8 mile and take the left fork for the next 3.4 miles. Go right at another fork for the final 0.8 mile to a parking

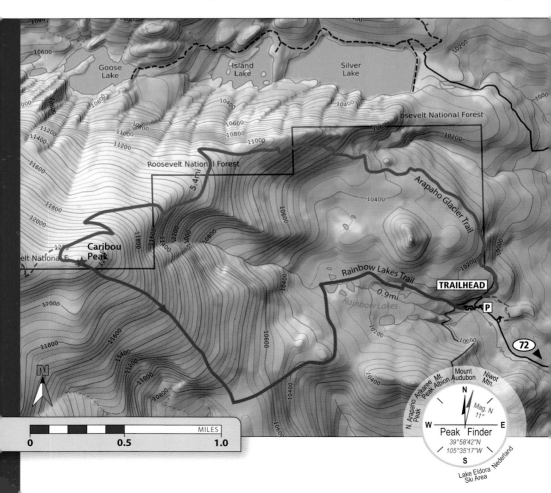

Caribou Peak from Rainbow Lakes.

area located on the right at the Arapaho Glacier trailhead. Regular cars can readily reach this trailhead.

COMMENTS: Look north from the summit to see the shimmering, green lakes that catch the silt out of the Arapaho Glacier. This peak is officially unnamed; "Caribou" is actually the annotation of the USGS benchmark on top.

That name comes from the nearby, former Caribou Mine and the ghost town of Caribou. Silver was mined in this area. For President Grant's visit to Central City in 1882, silver bricks were sent from Caribou to line the walkway to the Teller House. The town of Caribou had as many as 3,000 residents in the mid-1870s. But fires devastated the town on several occasions, and after the last in 1889, most residents moved on. The town site slowly drifted back to a natural state, with only a few foundations visible today.

THE ROUTE: The trail begins at the left side of the parking area at a sign stating, "Glacier Rim Trail, Arapaho Glacier Overlook 6 miles, Arapaho Pass Trail 8 miles." Follow this clear trail, generally north and then west, as it rises above timberline along the boundary of the Boulder watershed area, and then up the northern flank of Caribou Peak. About 100 feet below the top, leave the trail and ascend south to a huge cairn with an embedded metal pole. The only other marker on the summit is a small adjacent cairn.

WILD.
AREA

Descend by your ascent route. Or, if you would like to make a loop out of it, then descend southeast, along faint jeep trails across the tundra to near treeline. Pick up a trail here, descending northeast to Rainbow Lakes. Follow the trail around the north side of the lakes, as it tracks east, back to your trailhead.

49 Thunder Butte 9,836 Feet

DISTANCE: 3.0 miles each way

STARTING ELEVATION: 8,533 feet

ELEVATION GAIN: 1,919 feet (includes 383 extra feet)

HIKING TIME: Up in 123 minutes, down in 119 minutes (senior time)

TRAIL: Initial 0.25 mile and final 100 yards

SEASON: June to October

MAPS: Trails Illustrated #135

NEAREST LANDMARK: Deckers

GETTING THERE: From Deckers, where Jefferson 126 becomes CO-67, drive south on CO-67 for 9.0 miles and take a right turn toward Westcreek. After 300 yards turn left, pass the fire station, and turn onto Road 68. Pass Sheepnose Peak on the right and after about 2.0 miles, turn right on 9-J Road. If the road is open after 200 yards, drive 1.5 miles on this good dirt road and park on the right at an open meadow, with Thunder Butte visible.

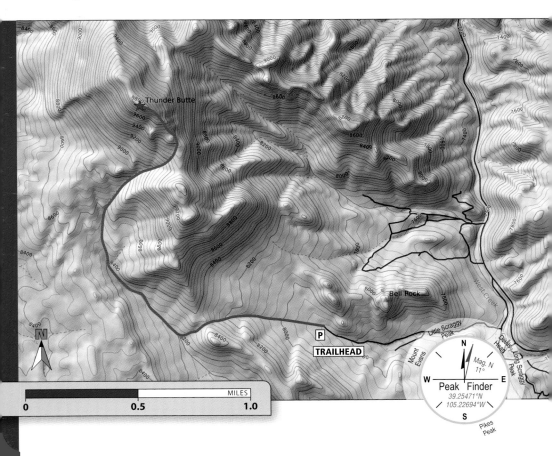

COMMENTS: This is the highest mountain in Douglas County and it is not a butte. Fallen trees and underbrush, remnants of the June 2002 Hayman Fire, increase the difficulty of this hike.

THE ROUTE: Begin north-northwest along a ridge with a narrow trail that ends after a few hundred yards. Gradually descend to a drainage and hike up on the right side of a large rock formation halfway up the peak and continue up to the ridge. Find a faint trail that leads to the base of the summit boulders. Ascend the right side of these rocks to a benchmark and a register. Enjoy the view before returning by your ascent route.

Thunder Butte and Pikes Peak from Cheesman Mountain.

50 Mount Trelease 12,477 Feet

DISTANCE: 3.2 miles each way

STARTING ELEVATION: 10,720 feet

ELEVATION GAIN: 2,021 feet (includes 132 feet extra each way)

HIKING TIME: Up in 125 minutes, down in 95 minutes

TRAIL: Initial 1.3 miles, bushwhack beyond

SEASON: Early June to early October

MAPS: Trails Illustrated #104

NEAREST LANDMARK: Bakerville

GETTING THERE: From I-70 between Bakerville and the Eisenhower-Johnson Tunnel, take Exit 216. The exit road passes south under I-70 on its way to Loveland Pass. Instead, quickly turn right (north and then northeast) and park alongside a neglected access road, blocked to vehicles in about 0.5 mile.

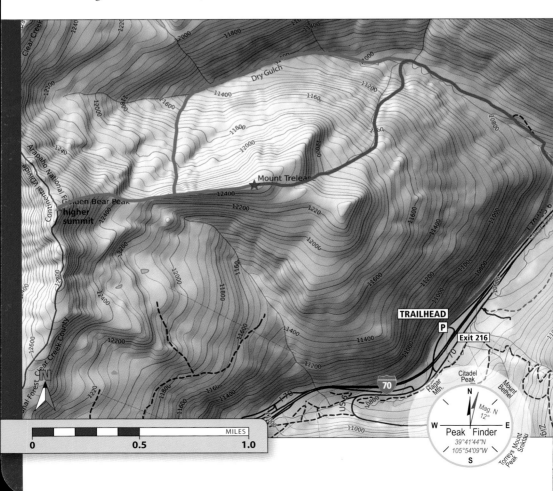

COMMENTS: The Eisenhower-Johnson Tunnel was cut through the southwestern flank of Mount Trelease. It is the highest automobile tunnel in the world. The summit of Mount Trelease overlooks the Loveland Basin Ski Area to the south and Loveland Valley Ski Area to the southeast.

This hike is to a sub-peak called Mount Trelease. But Golden Bear Peak is 0.5 mile west and some 500 feet higher. For extra credit, you may drop west off the summit and into a small saddle, before trudging up to Golden Bear on the Continental Divide in 1.2 miles. You can return by the same route or drop north from the saddle into Dry Gulch. Follow the gulch down to the east, avoiding most of the willows by crossing to the north side of the creek.

THE ROUTE: Proceed around the barrier and follow the access road northeast. You will pass two other barriers as the road rises, curves north and then northwest, and enters Dry Gulch. After the road ends, hike about 0.4 mile farther northwest, keeping to the right of the creek. There is only a faint trail from here onward. At about the 11,000-foot level, turn southwest, cross the creek and ascend Mount Trelease directly for about 1.0 mile, gaining about 1,500 feet. The summit is visible to the right of a smaller subpeak. The top has no special marking but a great view. Take the same route back to the trailhead.

Mount Trelease in the foreground with Golden Bear Peak on the left, as viewed from the south (Eric Wiseman).

51 Grizzly Peak 13,427 Feet

DISTANCE: 2.6 miles each way

STARTING ELEVATION: 11,990 feet (Loveland Pass)

ELEVATION GAIN: 2,387 feet (includes 475 feet extra each way)

HIKING TIME: Up in 122 minutes, down in 95 minutes

TRAIL: All the way, with occasional gaps

SEASON: Early June to early October

MAPS: Trails Illustrated #104

NEAREST LANDMARK: Loveland Pass

GETTING THERE: Drive to Loveland Pass on US-6, either south from I-70 via Exit 216 or west from Dillon and the Keystone resort area. Park at the summit of the pass on the east side of the highway.

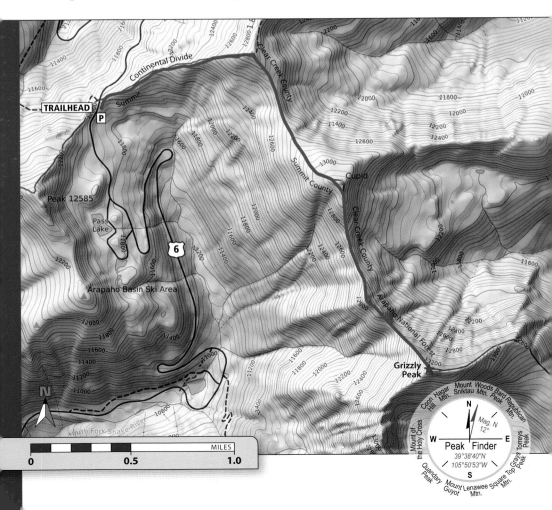

COMMENTS: Grizzly Peak and much of this hike are on the Continental Divide and the boundary between Clear Creek County and Summit County. This is a wonderful hike for those who enjoy ridge walking above timberline. The views are seemingly endless in all directions.

Get an early start, as the Colorado Rockies are infamous for brewing some fast-moving, afternoon thunderstorms. There have been several incidents on the ridges above Loveland Pass involving lightning. In each case, the hikers put themselves in jeopardy by staying high. If caught in the open on this ridge during an approaching storm, drop at least a few hundred feet off the ridge to wait things out.

THE ROUTE: Proceed up the ridge to the northeast on a clear trail. After 0.5 mile, leave this trail and turn right (southeast) before you reach the ridge. A trail passes in this direction, but is not essential to the hike. Contour until you eventually reach the ridge and

Looking down Chihuahua Gulch from the summit of Grizzly Peak.

continue southeast. You will lose elevation as you pass over or near several unnamed highpoints. The final saddle on the ridge lies 660 feet below the Grizzly Peak summit. A trail, present for most of the ridge, is very distinct on the scree for the final ascent. At the top is a semi-open rock shelter. The summit ridge extends toward Torreys Peak to the east. (The routes up that fourteener from this point, and from Chihuahua Gulch to the southeast, appear relatively easy.) Descend by your ascent route back to Loveland Pass, which can be seen throughout most of the hike.

CMC
CLASSIC
HIKE

52 Resolution Mountain 11,905 Feet

DISTANCE: 3.0 miles each way

STARTING ELEVATION: 11,905 feet

ELEVATION GAIN: 2,227 feet

HIKING TIME: Up in 120 minutes, down in 70 minutes

TRAIL: Initial 2.0 miles, bushwhack beyond

SEASON: Late May to mid-October

MAPS: Trails Illustrated #109

NEAREST LANDMARK: Leadville

GETTING THERE: Drive north of Leadville on US-24 from the intersection with CO-91 for 14.8 miles. Or if you come from the north, drive 15.2 miles south on US-24 from Minturn. Either of these routes brings you to a turnoff that goes east through two stone pillars into the former site of Camp Hale. After proceeding

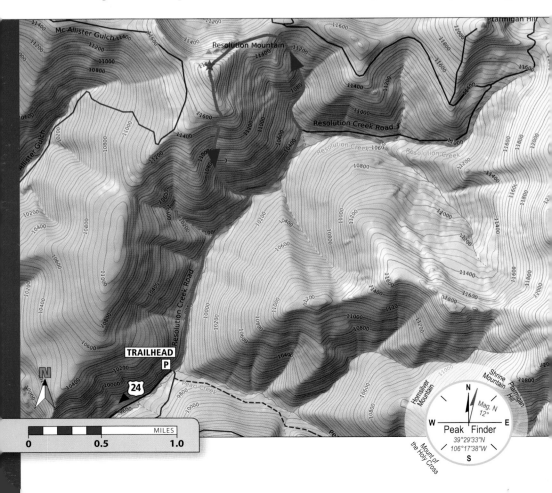

Approaching Resolution Mountain.

0.2 mile off US-24 through the pillars, turn left at a "T" and drive for 0.9 mile to a turnoff to the right and a creek crossing. You are now on Resolution Road #702. Keep on this road as it ascends northeast, alongside Resolution Creek, for 1.9 miles to a fork. You will want the left fork, often blocked to vehicles at this point. Park here.

COMMENTS: To reach the trailhead one must pass through the ruins of Camp Hale, which was established to train ski troops of the U.S. Army 10th Mountain Division for World War II and also as a camp for German prisoners of war. The Forest Service discourages on-foot exploration of the site because of possible unexploded ordinance.

THE ROUTE: Continue northeast on foot up the left-hand road along Resolution Creek for about 2.0 miles, where the road turns sharply to the right (east). Leave the road at this sharp bend and ascend up the gulch going northwest, keeping to the left of the creek. Stay left at the confluence of two creeks, continue northwest and gain the ridge at a low point. Then turn left (south) to the summit, which lies a total of 1.0 mile from where you left Resolution Road. At the top there is a metal pole marker and nearby, a cement slab with two embedded metal rods. To descend, you may retrace your route or make a loop by descending south to the unnamed creek that passes east through the aspen by way of an abandoned mine to Resolution Road.

(If Resolution Road is open to vehicles, a regular car can ascend to the sharp bend in the road at 10,382 feet. The hike can begin there and continue northwest, up the gulch away from the road. This would save 2.0 miles and 704 feet in elevation gain on the ascent.)

53 Teller Mountain 12,615 Feet

DISTANCE: 4.2 miles each way

STARTING ELEVATION: 10,830 feet

ELEVATION GAIN: 1,985 feet (includes 100 extra feet each way)

HIKING TIME: Up in 119 minutes, down in 92 minutes (senior time)

TRAIL: All the way until 10 yards from the summit

SEASON: June to October

MAPS: Trails Illustrated #104

NEAREST LANDMARK: Dillon

GETTING THERE: From US-6 at the Keystone Ski Area, drive up Montezuma Road and avoid sidetracks. Go through Montezuma. Continue up Deer Creek Road and park in a flat open area on the left after 7.0 miles from US-6 and 100 yards before an open wooden fence.

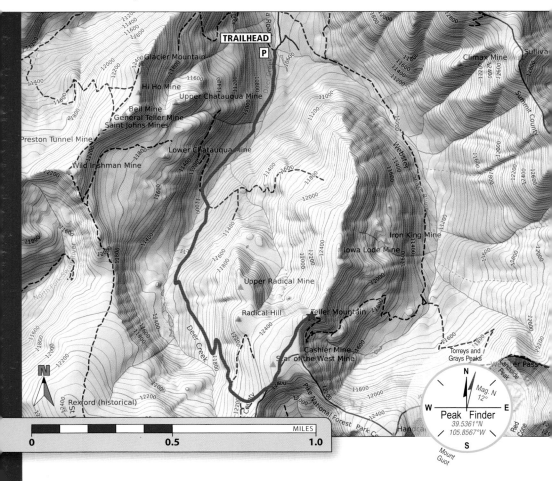

COMMENTS: The Bear Creek and Snake River area above Montezuma is full of popular four-wheel drive roads. This hike uses one of them to reach a wonderful 360-degree panorama of high peaks. The peak is named after Henry Teller, Colorado's first U.S. Senator.

THE ROUTE: Begin west up the road, pass the wood fencing and reach a fork after 0.6 mile. Go left on the road with a "Number 5" sign and gradually ascend the rough road. Pass a collection of logs off the road and reach a signed fork. Ascend left past treeline on Road 5. Stay on the rocky, wide main road and pass a poor trail on the left that leads toward Radical Hill. Reach another fork and a sign pointing right to Webster Pass and left to Radical Hill. Continue up straight ahead. Keep left and ascending as a right fork leads to Middle Deer Creek. The trail gradually rises to a high point on Teller Mountiain. This summit road continues down to the Snake River. There are high peaks visible in every direction. This is an exceptional viewing site. Avoid the temptation to shortcut back down and follow the rocky road back to your starting point.

The view west from the summit of Teller Mountain.

54 Twin Cones 12,060 & 12,058 Feet

DISTANCE: 5.2 miles each way

STARTING ELEVATION: 11,315 feet (Berthoud Pass)

ELEVATION GAIN: 1,976 feet (includes 900 extra feet)

HIKING TIME: Up to South Cone in 120 minutes, over to North Cone in 20 minutes, back in 115 minutes

TRAIL: Initial 1.2 miles

SEASON: Early June to early October

MAPS: Trails Illustrated #103

NEAREST LANDMARK: Empire

GETTING THERE: Drive on US-40 to Berthoud Pass and park in the large lot on the east side of the pass. Berthoud Pass connects Empire to the south with Winter Park to the north.

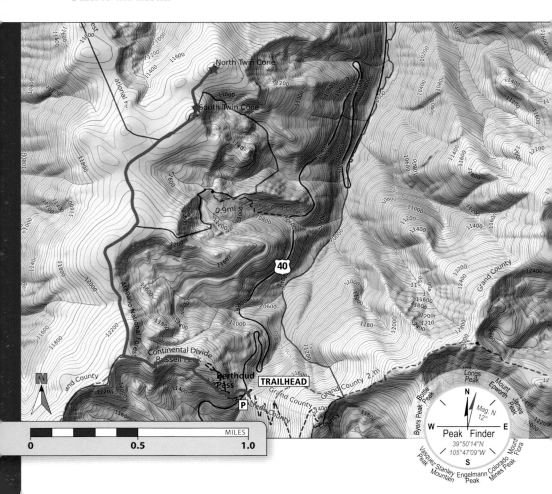

Twin Cones viewed from the south.

COMMENTS: Great views from each summit and an overlook of the Winter Park Ski Area are features of this long walk across the tundra.

THE ROUTE: Cross the highway and begin west on the Continental Divide Trail, which meanders up to a ridge at 12,391 feet in over 1.0 mile. Leave the trail and descend right (north) over tundra following cairns and poles that mark the route. The Twin Cones are visible ahead. After descending 350 feet, continue up over another ridge and a 250-foot decline before rising to the Twin Cones, which are 0.5 mile apart. The North Cone is part of the Winter Park Ski Area and the South Cone summit is a huge boulder. Return as you ascended.

WILD.
AREA

55 Mount Bethel 12,705 Feet

DISTANCE: 2.75 miles on ascent, 1.5 miles on descent

STARTING ELEVATION: 10,600 feet

ELEVATION GAIN: 2,125 feet (includes 10 extra feet each way)

HIKING TIME: Up in 93 minutes, down in 54 minutes

TRAIL: Initial 1.9 miles on ascent, final 1.0 mile on descent

SEASON: Early June to early October

MAPS: Trails Illustrated #104

NEAREST LANDMARK: Bakerville

GETTING THERE: From I-70, between Bakerville and the Eisenhower-Johnson Tunnel, take Exit 216. The exit road passes south under I-70 on its way to Loveland Pass. Instead, quickly turn right (north and then northeast) and park alongside a neglected access road, blocked to vehicles in about 0.5 mile.

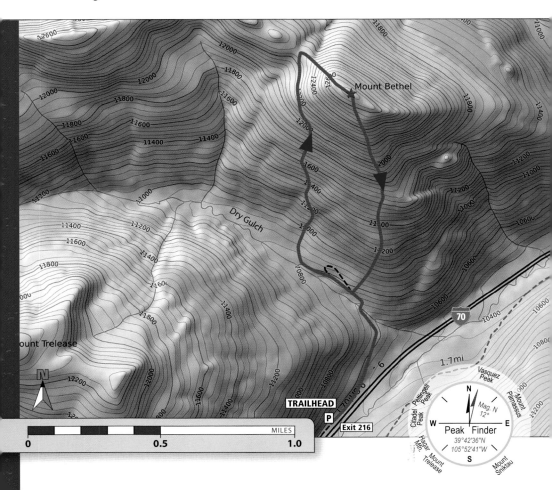

Mount Bethel from along the frontage road.

COMMENTS: The triangular top of this mountain dominates the western horizon as one drives from Bakerville on I-70 toward Loveland Basin. The snow fences protect I-70 from snow accumulating in the obvious avalanche chute that faces the highway. Mount Bethel lies between Dry Gulch to the southeast and Herman Gulch to the northeast.

Formerly called Little Professor Peak, Mount Bethel was renamed to honor Ellsworth Bethel, a pathologist with the U.S. Department of Agriculture who, while a leader in the Colorado Mountain Club, named several Front Range summits, including the Indian Peaks.

THE ROUTE: Walk northeast on the frontage road as it ascends and curves north and then northwest into Dry Gulch. The road is blocked to vehicles, but accessible on foot.

As you enter the basin, Mount Bethel will be visible on your right and is distinguishable by two rows of snow barricades on its southwest flank. At road end, keep a few hundred yards to the right of Dry Creek and soon begin to hike up and north toward the saddle west of Mount Bethel. Before you reach the saddle, angle steeply northeast, gain the ridge, and proceed to the cairn at the summit. Some easy hand work may be necessary, just before the ridge, but there is no special risk.

The descent can be made more directly due south to the place where the road ended on your ascent. Aim downhill, passing between the snow fences. Once you reach the trees, it is steep but easy going through the scattered forest down to the road.

56 Hornsilver Mountain 11,572 Feet

DISTANCE: 4.0 miles each way

STARTING ELEVATION: 9,020 feet

ELEVATION GAIN: 2,552 feet

HIKING TIME: Up in 120 minutes, down in 100 minutes

TRAIL: All the way

SEASON: Late May to mid-October

MAPS: Trails Illustrated #108 & 109

NEAREST LANDMARK: Redcliff

GETTING THERE: From US-24, about 9.5 miles south of the intersection with I-70, turn east toward the town of Redcliff. From Redcliff, take the Shrine Pass Road and drive up toward Shrine Pass for 2.45 miles and park. Alternately, drive west

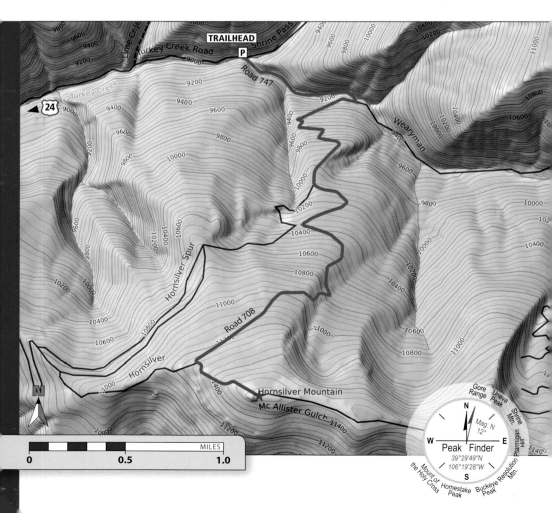

over Shrine Pass toward Redcliff from the Shrine Pass cutoff of I-70 (Exit #190) for a total of 8.5 miles. Park here off the road, as the side road to Hornsilver Mountain requires four-wheel drive.

The view of Mount of the Holy Cross from Hornsilver Mountain.

COMMENTS: Hornsilver's flat, grassy summit affords excellent views to the west of the famous cross of snow on Mount of the Holy Cross. Certainly that peak is one of the most famous peaks in Colorado and a prime target for climbers of the fourteeners. The mountain and its mysterious cross were the subject of rumors for much of the 19th century, until W. H. Jackson confirmed its existence with his famous photograph in 1873. After a USGS survey in the 1950s determined that the peak just barely qualified as a fourteener, peakbaggers took renewed interest.

Four-wheel drive can take you to the top of Hornsilver Mountain, and also to near the top of adjacent Resolution Mountain to the south, by way of the same road. For an easier crossing of Wearyman Creek, this hike is best done in late August or September. However for prime viewing of the cross, early summer is best, before the snow melts.

THE ROUTE: Leave Shrine Pass Road and hike south on Road 747. Follow this rough road for 0.65 mile, crossing Wearyman Creek at several points and taking the right fork onto Road 708. Follow this road up, and generally south, in a counterclockwise direction to the flat, grassy summit at timberline. A few rocks, old boards and wire mark the high point, just west of the road. Return by the same route.

57 Bald Mountain (Summit County) 13,684 Feet

DISTANCE: 2.0 miles each way

STARTING ELEVATION: 11,390 feet

ELEVATION GAIN: 2,602 feet (includes 154 feet lost between summits)

HIKING TIME: Up in 130 minutes, down in 90 minutes

TRAIL: None, all off-trail on tundra and talus

SEASON: July to early October

MAPS: Trails Illustrated #109

NEAREST LANDMARK: Breckenridge

GETTING THERE: Drive to the south end of the town of Breckenridge on US-9 and turn east onto Summit County Road 10, the Boreas Pass Road. The pavement ends in 3.5 miles. Continue driving on the road for a total of 9.65 miles toward Boreas Pass. Park at the bend in the road, 0.6 mile short of the pass. From the southeast,

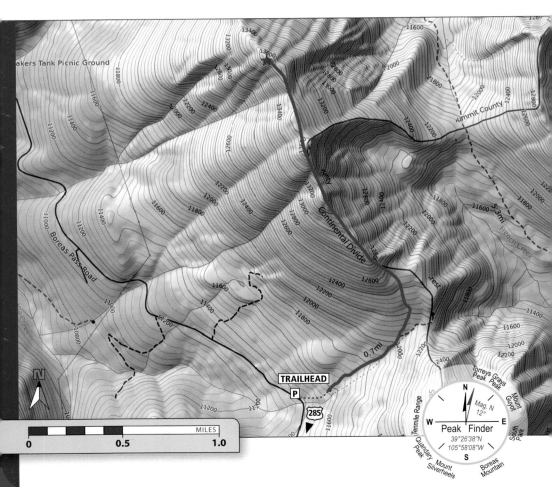

this trailhead can be reached by turning west off US-285, 10.0 miles north of Fairplay, onto Boreas Pass Road (Park County Road 33). Drive through the town of Como for a total of 11.3 miles to the pass. The trailhead is 0.6 mile farther north beyond the pass. Regular cars can easily traverse Boreas Pass when there is no blockage by snow. Park off the road.

Bald Mountain from the summit of Mount Boreas.

COMMENTS: This is a good hike for those who enjoy ridge walking and being above timberline. Boreas Pass, now named for the God of the North Wind, had been called Hamilton, Tarryall, and then Breckenridge Pass. In 1882, track was laid over the pass and it was a Denver, South Park and Pacific Railroad Company route until 1937. A town called Boreas was located at the pass for the railroad workers and travelers. This was the highest post office in the country in 1898.

A restored, 1882 Section House stands on top of the pass. It hosts visitors as part of the Summit Huts Association.

THE ROUTE: Head northeast and up, staying to the left of the creek, and quickly pass timberline. Proceed to the ridge at the left of the saddle, between Bald Mountain on your left and Boreas Mountain on your right. This saddle is known as Black Powder Pass. Ascend this ridge toward Bald Mountain and traverse several false summits, heading north. The true summit is marked by a large cairn and a circular rock shelter. Two other large cairns lie farther to the northwest, down from the summit. To descend, stay on the summit ridge and keep to the west (right) of the last two false summits, returning as you came up.

58 Mount Wilcox 13,408 Feet
Otter Mountain 12,766 Feet

DISTANCE: 1.95 miles to Mount Wilcox, 1.85 miles from Mount Wilcox to Otter Mountain, 2.0 miles from Otter Mountain to trailhead

STARTING ELEVATION: 11,594 feet

ELEVATION GAIN: 2,394 feet

HIKING TIME: 116 minutes to Mt. Wilcox, 46 minutes from Mt. Wilcox to Otter Mountain, 68 minutes from Otter Mountain to trailhead

TRAIL: Initial 0.5 mile, off-trail tundra and talus beyond

SEASON: Mid-June to early October

MAPS: Trails Illustrated #104

NEAREST LANDMARK: Georgetown

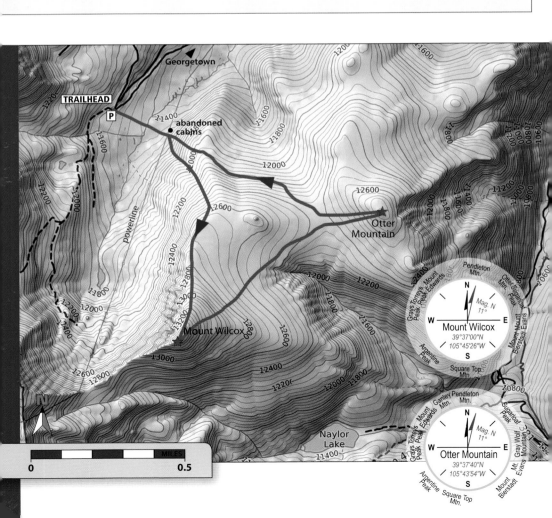

GETTING THERE: From the intersection of Sixth and Rose Streets in Georgetown, drive south and up toward Guanella Pass for 2.8 miles to a dirt road on your right. Turn onto this road, take the right fork at 0.25 mile, another right fork at 0.5 mile and also at 1.0 mile from the paved road. In 0.2 mile farther, take the sharp left fork and continue up the basin for a total of 6.25 miles from Guanella Pass Road to the substantial ruins of the Waldorf Mine, just above timberline. Park here. Although this road can be quite rough in spots, passenger cars with good clearance can usually negotiate the road to this point. Mount Wilcox is the prominent peak to the southwest.

Mount Wilcox from Silver Dollar Lake.

COMMENTS: Mount Wilcox was named on August 1, 1948, after Edward John Wilcox, who owned the nearby Waldorf Mines. In fact, the ghost town of Waldorf was once called Wilcox. A railroad that ran up Mount McClellan opened on August 12, 1906, and passed through Waldorf, which then was called the site of the highest post office in the United States. The train line could only operate three months out of each year and was eventually torn up in 1919.

THE ROUTE: Go east over Leavenworth Creek to two abandoned cabins on the east side of the creek near some power lines—follow an old mining road across the creek and through the marshes toward these cabins, thereby avoiding most of the scrub oak on the basin floor. The trail ends at the cabins. Continue steeply up to the east for 1.3 miles to gain the ridge. Turn south and soon the Mount Wilcox summit will come into view. Cross the tundra and ascend easily to a large summit cairn.

Continue this loop hike by descending from Mount Wilcox and heading northeast to Otter Mountain. Keep to the south of an unnamed peak with a rocky wind shelter on top. This peak lies about halfway between Mount Wilcox and Otter Mountain. Continue northeast over the gently rising tundra to another large cairn at the Otter Mountain summit. Descend directly west to the ridge, then to the two cabins and pick up the old road back across Leavenworth Creek to your car.

59 Fletcher Mountain 13,951 Feet

DISTANCE: 3.2 miles each way

STARTING ELEVATION: 11,718 feet

ELEVATION GAIN: 2,443 feet (includes an extra 105 feet each way)

HIKING TIME: Up in 127 minutes, down in 107 minutes

TRAIL: Initial 2.0 miles, intermittent and faint thereafter

SEASON: July to October

MAPS: Trails Illustrated #109

NEAREST LANDMARK: Breckenridge

GETTING THERE: From the traffic light in Breckenridge at Ski Hill Road, drive south on CO-9 for 7.9 miles and turn right at a curve in the road onto Summit County Road 850. Keep straight after 0.1 mile and again after another 0.1 mile. Go right at mile 1.3 and left at mile 2.2 and park near the road barrier just below the dam at Upper Blue Lake. Regular cars can drive this far.

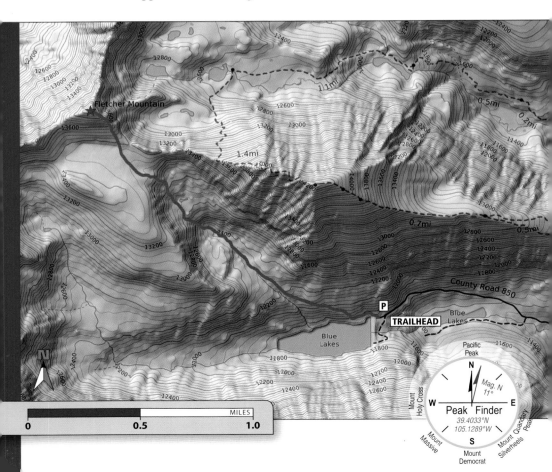

Fletcher Mountain (right) and Drift Peak (left) from the summit of Atlantic Peak.

COMMENTS: Fletcher Mountain is one of Colorado's 100 highest peaks. For such a high mountain it is relatively easy to reach the summit. Towering mountains abound in this area and great views are available from the top. Most of this hike is above timberline.

THE ROUTE: Start from the road barrier and ascend to the dam at Upper Blue Lake. A trail begins at the north end of the paved walkway above the dam. Follow this trail and within 75 yards, steeply ascend the right fork. The trail then curves to the northwest up a valley. At 1.25 miles from the trailhead you pass the remnants of two wooden cabins. There are two trails that rise northwest into the basin—I recommend the trail to the left of the creek. After about 0.5 mile from the cabin ruins, the trail ends. Find a route up northwest to a vast, flat area of grass and rock. Fletcher Mountain lies ahead to the northwest. Hike up to the ridge to the right of the summit and follow the ridge west to the top. A rock pile and register cylinder are at the high point. Generally retrace your route back to the trailhead.

60 Bergen Peak 9,708 Feet

DISTANCE: 4.6 miles each way

STARTING ELEVATION: 7,760 feet

ELEVATION GAIN: 2,708 feet (includes 380 feet extra each way)

HIKING TIME: Up in 120 minutes, down in 80 minutes

TRAIL: All the way

SEASON: Mid-April to late November

MAPS: Trails Illustrated #100; Elk Meadow Park Map

NEAREST LANDMARK: Evergreen

GETTING THERE: From I-70 take Exit 252, cross over I-70, and from the first stoplight drive south 5.3 miles, or drive north from Evergreen on CO-74 from the junction with Jefferson County Road 73 for 2.1 miles. Then turn west onto Stage Coach Boulevard, and in 1.1 miles, park on the right (north) in the trailhead parking area.

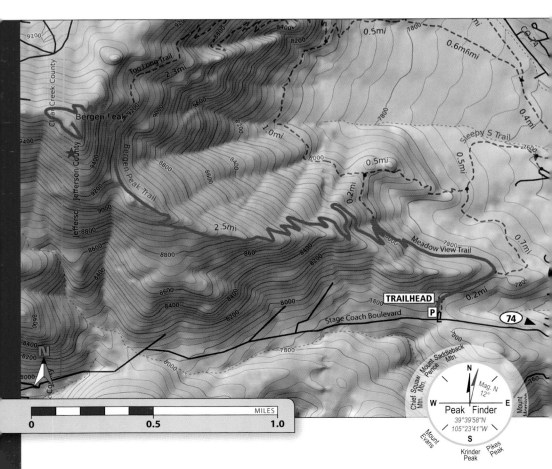

COMMENTS: Bergen Peak is named after Thomas C. Bergen, who came from Illinois seeking gold and settled west of Denver in 1859. His combined hotel and post office was a busy spot along the toll road west from Mount Vernon. He was one of the first three Jefferson County Commissioners.

Near the summit there are fine views of the Mount Evans massif as it shimmers above the foreground foothill peaks. There are several other enjoyable trails in this Jefferson County Open Space Park, free and open to the public. If you bring your dog, enjoy the designated off-leash area in a pretty meadow south of the parking lot, complete with water for cooling off.

The summit of Bergen Peak.

THE ROUTE: Proceed to the northeast on a trail, past the picnic tables and toilets, to a junction in 0.3 miles. Take the left fork and continue along the Meadow View Trail for 0.6 miles. Then at another fork, go left again and head west, and then northwest, on the Bergen Peak Trail for 2.7 miles. Yet another left fork leads you in a counterclockwise route of one more mile to the Bergen Peak summit. The trail passes a scenic overlook and soon curves left. Leave the trail and ascend the ridge on the left for 150 yards to a summit sign at the high point.

CMC
CLASSIC
HIKE

Take the same route back. If you want more exercise or variety, head back to the first trail intersection, 1.0 mile down from the summit, and take the left fork onto the Too Long Trail. This trail eventually curves around to connect with the beginning segments of your ascent route.

61 Raleigh Peak 8,183 Feet

DISTANCE: 6.0 miles each way

STARTING ELEVATION: 6,120 feet

ELEVATION GAIN: 2,523 feet (includes 230 feet extra each way)

HIKING TIME: Up in 185 minutes, down in 127 minutes

TRAIL: Initial 80%

SEASON: Mid-April to mid-November

MAPS: Trails Illustrated #135

NEAREST LANDMARK: Buffalo Creek

GETTING THERE: From US-285 west of Conifer, drive south on Foxton Road (Jefferson 97), which passes through Reynolds Park. After 8.3 miles from US-285, turn left on Jefferson 96, which runs parallel to the North Fork of the South Platte River. Six miles on this road takes you past the abandoned South Platte Hotel to a sign, a bridge, and a parking area on the right.

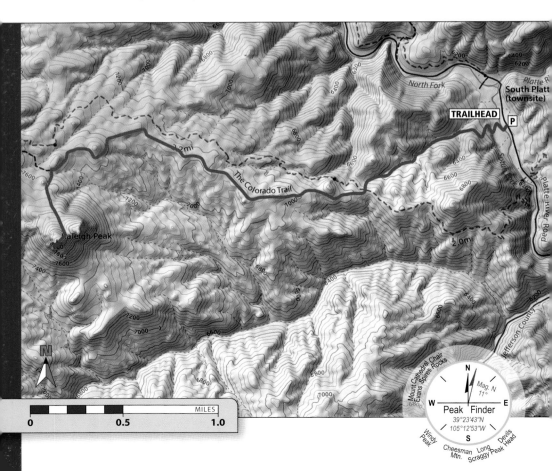

Raleigh Peak from the northeast.

COMMENTS: This is a good early or late season hike with an interesting, rocky summit. The route, after leaving the trail, is faint and may require some bushwhacking and compass work. The Hayman Fire of 2002 claimed many trees, thus enabling great views along this hike.

The fine footbridge over the Platte at the start of this hike is named for Gudy Gaskill, the "mother" of the Colorado Trail. This spot is the start of Segment 2 of the 468-mile, Denver to Durango trail.

THE ROUTE: From the parking area, cross the South Platte River on the long, sturdy footbridge. On the opposite bank, descend to the level of the river and wrap back under the bridge to the southeast. The trail then rises out of the canyon in a series of switchbacks to a high plateau with vast vistas. After 2.0 miles leave the Colorado Trail and go left on a service road. Follow this road until rocky Raleigh Peak is directly to the south. Leave the road and bushwhack down to the foot of the peak. Then ascend through a burn area to the ridge on the right and then follow the ridge up to the left. Some easy hand work may be needed near the bare rocky summit. The best return is to retrace your outward bound route.

62 Ganley Mountain 12,902 Feet
Pendleton Mountain 12,275 Feet

DISTANCE: 4.3 miles to Ganley Mountain,
 1.7 miles from Ganley Mountain to Pendleton Mtn., 5.5 miles on return

STARTING ELEVATION: 11,594 feet

ELEVATION GAIN: 1,808 feet (includes 500 feet extra on return)

HIKING TIME: Up Ganley Mtn. in 145 minutes,
 Ganley Mountain to Pendleton Mtn. in 40 minutes, down in 140 minutes

TRAIL: Initial 2.5 miles

SEASON: Mid-June to early October

MAPS: Trails Illustrated #104

NEAREST LANDMARK: Georgetown

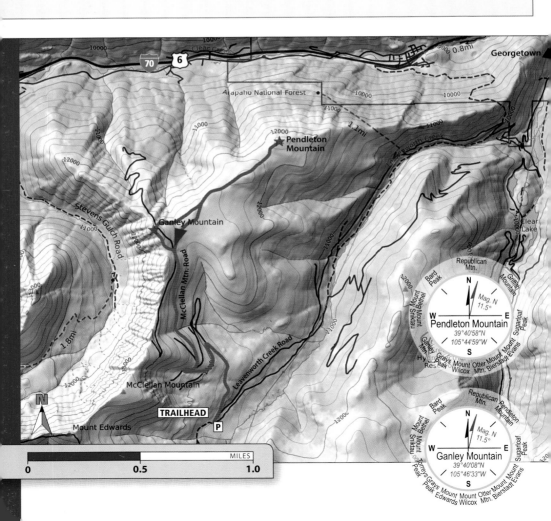

GETTING THERE: From the intersection of Sixth and Rose Streets in Georgetown, drive south and up toward Guanella Pass for 2.8 miles to a dirt road on your right. Turn off onto this road, take the right fork at 0.25 mile, another right fork at 0.5 mile and also at 1.0 mile from the paved road. In 0.2 mile farther, take the sharp left fork and continue up the basin for a total of 6.25 miles from Guanella Pass Road to the substantial ruins of the Waldorf Mine, just above timberline. Park here. Although this road can be quite rough in spots, passenger cars with good clearance can usually make it to this point.

COMMENTS: This hike is completely above timberline with rewarding views of two famous fourteeners. Ganley Mountain is named for John W. Ganley, the first postmaster of Silver Plume. Pendleton Mountain is named after George H. Pendleton, the vice presidential running mate of General George McClellan on the unsuccessful Democratic ticket of 1864.

Heading towards Pendleton Mountain. (Eric Wiseman)

THE ROUTE: Begin hiking north up the road. After 0.65 mile, take the right fork. Just beyond, at a four-way intersection, continue straight (north). In 0.3 mile, take the right fork and a sharp left fork in 0.3 more miles. The road continues in switchbacks. In 0.6 mile, take the right fork and again 0.1 mile later. In another 1.4 miles, take another right fork and soon thereafter, leave the road and ascend to the left (northwest) over tundra to the summit of Ganley Mountain. A small cairn sits at the top. The view southwest to Stevens Gulch and two fourteeners, Grays and Torreys Peaks, is especially rewarding.

Descend northeast, losing about 600 feet over the 1.7 miles of tundra to the top of Pendleton Mountain. Note that this peak is lower than the intervening high points. A small cairn marks the summit.

Return to your car at the Waldorf Mine site as you ascended, passing slightly below the summit of Ganley Mountain. Be sure on the drive back down Leavenworth Gulch to take the sharp right fork after 5.0 miles from Waldorf.

63 Horseshoe Mountain 13,898 Feet

DISTANCE: 3.1 miles each way

STARTING ELEVATION: 11,800 feet

ELEVATION GAIN: 2,218 feet (includes 60 extra feet each way)

HIKING TIME: Up in 106 minutes, down in 82 minutes (senior time)

TRAIL: All the way

SEASON: July to mid-October

MAPS: Trails Illustrated#110

NEAREST LANDMARK: Fairplay

GETTING THERE: Drive south on US-285 from Fairplay from the junction with CO-9 for 1.25 miles. Then turn right (west) on Park County Road 18 (also called Fourmile Creek Road) and continue up the valley on the main road for 10.2 miles to the site of the former Leavick Mine. Drive 0.8 mile farther on the main road

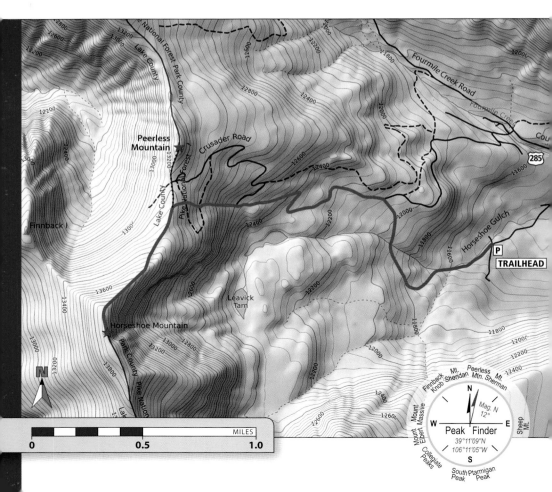

Horsehoe Mountain and Mount Sheridan rom Sheep Mountain.

and go left on Road 603. Keep left at a fork and park 0.3 mile from Fourmile Road. A snowfield often blocks this road at this point. Regular cars should be able to make it this far.

COMMENTS: Horseshoe Mountain is very hiker friendly with the wide gradual road to the summit ridge trail. As you drive west on Fourmile Creek Road, you pass the site of the former town of Horseshoe, which once had a population as high as 800 and was called East Leadville.

This hike lies totally above timberline and takes you through many abandoned mines to an extensive view from the summit, which divides Park from Lake County. Horseshoe Mountain is named after its configuration, with a nearly perfect, glacier-carved cirque on its east face. The peak has added significance because it is one of the 100 highest peaks in Colorado, and a coveted mountain for peakbaggers.

Horseshoe Mountain from the east.

THE ROUTE: Follow the wide road as it curls up west into Horseshoe Gulch. The impressive Horseshoe Mountain cirque lies before you. Switchbacks bring you up past remnants of the Peerless Mine to road end at the ridge. Follow the occasionally faint trail south 0.8 mile to a summit rock pile. An old mining cabin sits a few hundred yards south on the ridge. Enjoy the views, and on your return you may want to use some of the alternate roads and take shortcuts back to the main road.

64 Whale Peak 13,078 Feet

DISTANCE: 4.0 miles each way
STARTING ELEVATION: 10,316 feet
ELEVATION GAIN: 2,832 feet (includes 35 feet extra each way)
HIKING TIME: Up in 148 minutes, down in 95 minutes
TRAIL: Most of the way, faint in places
SEASON: Early June to early October
MAPS: Trails Illustrated #104
NEAREST LANDMARK: Grant

GETTING THERE: From US-285 at the ghost town of Webster (4.4 miles east of Kenosha Pass or 3.25 miles west of Grant), turn west on Road 120 and drive up Hall Valley for 5.3 miles, past the Handcart Campground, to the Hall Valley Campground. En route, take the right fork at 3.3 miles and the left fork at 5.2 miles from

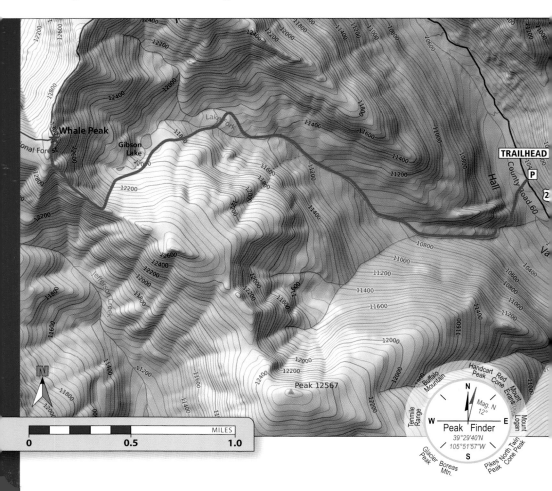

Whale Peak.

US-285. Continue on the rough road up the valley for 1.25 more miles past the Hall Valley Campground to a parking area on the left. Park here. Regular cars can usually make it this far.

COMMENTS: Whale Peak lies on the Continental Divide, on the boundary between Park and Summit Counties and also between Pike and Arapaho National Forests. The Hall Valley is named after Colonel William Jairus Hall, a local mine owner.

Whale Peak is an excellent hike in late September when the aspen stands of the Hall Valley are at their golden peak and the tundra above Gibson Lake turns to a deep, autumn crimson.

THE ROUTE: Follow the trail, which begins west of the parking area at a sign. Descend slightly to the south, cross the creek on a small wooden bridge and proceed southwest, and then west, up the valley on the clear trail, keeping to the right of the Lake Fork of the South Platte River until you cross it near timberline. After 1.7 miles from the trailhead, take the left fork, staying lower in the valley and closer to the creek. Avoid the right fork, which ascends steeply into the northern edge of the basin. After 1.6 miles past the fork, you will arrive at Gibson Lake. If you lose the trail, just continue close to the creek and toward the southwest corner of the basin and Gibson Lake. Pass to the left of the lake and ascend talus and tundra on the south to gain a trail leading to a saddle on the southwest ridge of Whale Peak. Then continue northwest up this ridge to the summit cairn. Descend as you came up.

65 Sugarloaf Peak 12,513 Feet

DISTANCE: 4.4 miles each way

STARTING ELEVATION: 9,640 feet

ELEVATION GAIN: 3,073 feet (includes 100 feet extra each way)

HIKING TIME: Up in 142 minutes, down in 96 minutes

TRAIL: Initial 2.8 miles, bushwhacking and tundra walking beyond

SEASON: Early June to early October

MAPS: Trails Illustrated #104

NEAREST LANDMARK: Idaho Springs

GETTING THERE: From Exit 240 off I-70 at Idaho Springs, drive southwest on CO-103 for 6.7 miles. At a sharp bend in the highway, Road 114, also called West Chicago Creek Road, leads southwest. Follow this excellent dirt road until it ends after 3.0 miles in a parking area, just past the West Chicago Creek Campground. Park here.

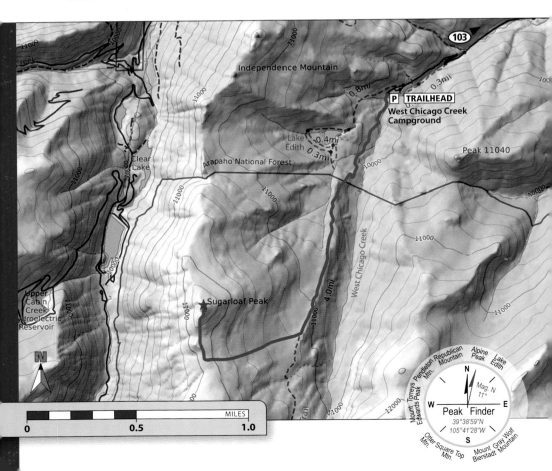

COMMENTS: Several Colorado Mountains are named Sugarloaf Peak due to their conical configuration. This peak can be seen from the northern segments of Guanella Pass Road and from numerous Clear Creek County high points. Nearby Lake Edith lies within private property. A loop return from the summit to the northeast, via an old mining road and Lake Edith, is therefore not recommended.

Your route lies within the magnificent Mount Evans Wilderness Area, offering several unique features worthy of a visit. Rare south of the Arctic Circle, the wilderness contains small pockets of arctic tundra. Unlike typical Colorado alpine tundra that is dry and brittle once the snow recedes, arctic tundra holds numerous small pools of water. Mountain goats, introduced in the 1940s, gambol on Gray Wolf Mountain, across the basin from Sugarloaf to the southeast. The area also holds two popular fourteeners—Mount Evans and Mount Bierstadt.

Sugarloaf Peak viewed from the north.

WILD.
AREA

THE ROUTE: The trail begins at a sign at the south end of the parking area. Follow this clear trail as it ascends to the south. After 2.3 miles leave the trail and bushwhack west-southwest to the saddle at the left (south) of Sugarloaf Peak. Ascend through sparse forest, willows, and scrub to the ridge. Then travel north-northwest over tundra to the summit, which is marked by a red and white pole embedded in a rock pile and with a nearby USGS marker in the midst of a smaller pile of rocks. Descend by your ascent route.

66 Quail Mountain 13,461 Feet

DISTANCE: 3.1 miles each way

STARTING ELEVATION: 9,870 feet

ELEVATION GAIN: 3,651 feet (includes 30 feet extra each way)

HIKING TIME: Up in 140 minutes, down in 90 minutes

TRAIL: Initial 2.4 miles, off-trail tundra beyond

SEASON: Late June to early October

MAPS: Trails Illustrated #127 & 129

NEAREST LANDMARK: Buena Vista

GETTING THERE: Drive west on Chaffee County Road 390 from US-24 between Leadville and Buena Vista. This road is 4.3 miles south of CO-82 and 15.3 miles north of the stoplight in Buena Vista (at CO-306). On this good dirt road, keep left at mile 3.5 and at mile 6.0. Pass the ghost town of Vicksburg at mile 8.0. Just past a pond and a campsite on the left at mile 9.4, the trailhead sign stating "Colorado Trail" is off the right side of the road. Park around here.

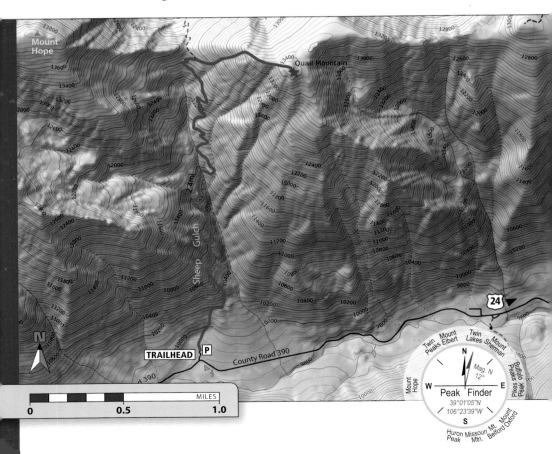

Quail Mountain viewed from Mount Hope.

COMMENTS: Quail Mountain is the location of a proposed ski area in the Twin Lakes area. This peak has a gentle, rounded summit that provides extensive views of many high mountains, including several fourteeners and Colorado's highest peak, Mount Elbert, to the northwest.

From the saddle to the west, Mount Hope, one of the 100 highest peaks in Colorado, is an easy 2 miles west from the saddle. The trail over this saddle is no longer the official route of the Colorado Trail. The actual route has been relocated on the east side of Quail Mountain. However, the Colorado Trail Foundation still lists this route as a strenuous, optional route for backpackers interested in getting a taste of Colorado's alpine.

THE ROUTE: Begin north on the trail, which leads steeply up into Sheep Gulch. On the way, you will soon pass an abandoned mine shaft on the left, and higher in the gulch, an old cabin lies off the trail on your right. Around timberline, the trail is marked by a series of cairns as it rises with switchbacks to the saddle between Mount Hope on your left (west) and Quail Mountain on your right (east). From this saddle at 12,530 feet, leave the trail and ascend 0.7 mile east over tundra to the top of Quail Mountain. Return as you ascended.

67

Mount Manitou 9,460 Feet
Rocky Mountain 9,250 Feet

DISTANCE: 3.4 miles to Mt. Manitou, 0.5 mile Mt. Manitou to Rocky Mountain,
3.3 miles from Rocky Mountain to trailhead

STARTING ELEVATION: 6,680 feet

ELEVATION GAIN: 3,060 feet

HIKING TIME: Up to Mt. Manitou in 120 minutes, Mt. Manitou to Rocky Mtn.
in 33 minutes, down from Rocky Mtn. in 83 minutes

TRAIL: Most of the way, off-trail close to top of Mt. Manitou and between summits,
plus some easy scrambling

SEASON: Late April to late November

MAPS: Trails Illustrated #137

NEAREST LANDMARK: Manitou Springs

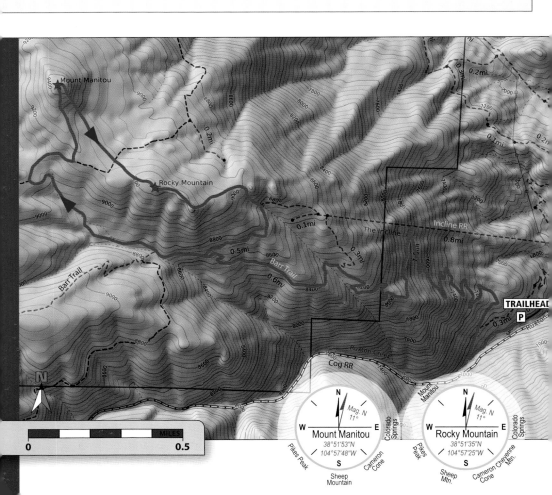

GETTING THERE: From Manitou Avenue in the town of Manitou Springs (west of Colorado Springs), drive southwest up Ruxton Avenue for 0.8 mile to the end of the public road. Turn right (northwest) and go 0.1 mile to a parking area, restrooms, and a bulletin board adjacent to the trailhead. Park here.

COMMENTS: The first part of this loop hike involves the historic Barr Trail, which is the major hiking route to the top of Pikes Peak. This trail, completed by Fred Barr in 1921, is extensively maintained and includes Barr Camp, an overnight accommodation at about the halfway point.

THE ROUTE: Follow the Barr Trail steeply up and to the west in a series of switch-backs. The trail is very well maintained and has wooden fencing along it for most of the first 2.0 miles. After about 80 minutes, you will reach a fork. Continue to the left (west) on the Barr Trail. In about five more minutes, another fork at a metal sign is reached. Take the right fork toward the former Fremont Experimental Forest

Mount Manitou from Rocky Mountain.

and leave the Barr Trail. After passing some old cement foundations on your right in 17 minutes from the Barr Trail, you arrive at a saddle and a "T." Take the right fork, going northeast, and ascend another seven minutes, before leaving the old road and proceeding due north to Mount Manitou. Near the top, some easy scrambling is necessary. At the tree-covered summit, there is a large rock with a register jar on top.

To reach Rocky Mountain, descend toward the southeast and stay close to the ill-defined ridge. Cross the old road that you left earlier and continue generally east and upward, past a false summit, to reach the treeless, rocky top of Rocky Mountain. Reaching the high point requires the careful use of hands. A board and iron rod mark the summit.

Descend Rocky Mountain to the east and pick up a faint trail that winds past some rocky projections, reaching the upper terminus of the former Mount Manitou Incline Railway in about 15 minutes. (If you find no trail, just continue east.) From there, take the trail west and upward 150 feet, leading to the Barr Trail. After nine minutes, take the left fork, descend and reach the fork that meets the Barr Trail in four more minutes. Turn left (east) and descend on the trail on which you ascended, reaching the trailhead in 55 minutes.

68 Buffalo Mountain 13,164 Feet

DISTANCE: 1.8 miles each way

STARTING ELEVATION: 9,560 feet

ELEVATION GAIN: 3,217 feet

HIKING TIME: Up in 150 minutes, down in 90 minutes

TRAIL: Most of the way, talus and tundra beyond

SEASON: Mid-June to early October

MAPS: Trails Illustrated #108

NEAREST LANDMARK: Silverthorne

GETTING THERE: From I-70, take Exit #205 (the Dillon-Silverthorne exit) and drive northwest about one block. Turn left (south) onto Wildernest Road. Follow this road, which becomes Ryan Gulch Road, passing through an area of condominiums, for 3.5 miles to the trailhead on the right (north), at a sign stating "Buffalo Cabin Trail." Park off the left (south) side of the road at a National Forest bulletin board.

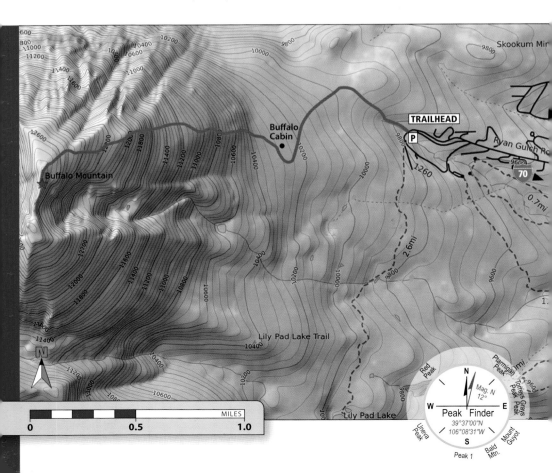

COMMENTS: There are a number of Buffalo Mountains in Colorado (but no buffaloes, just bison). This one is the dome that dominates the western view from the Eisenhower-Johnson Tunnel. The trail is a bit steep, but the view of Lake Dillon and rough Gore Range from the top is truly exceptional.

Mountain goats patrol the rugged north slopes of Buffalo Mountain. Even if you are not lucky enough to spot one, you may find a tuft of coarse, white fur, left from shedding their winter coats, stuck in the summit rocks.

Buffalo Mountain from the south.

THE ROUTE: Cross Ryan Gulch Road and proceed northwest on the Buffalo Cabin Trail. In 15 minutes take a left fork, and a minute later you arrive at a four-way intersection. A severe right turn takes you to Mesa Cortina. A milder right turn leads to Willow Creek. Take the left trail however, which goes past a ruined cabin on the right in twelve minutes, and five minutes later, to the ruined, so-called, Buffalo Cabin. You now have a choice of two routes to the top of Buffalo Mountain. A trail to the left of Buffalo Cabin passes steeply up through the trees to the west, over considerable scree and loose rocks. This trail ends above timberline, as the summit comes into view on your left (south). The other choice is a trail that begins to the right of Buffalo Cabin and continues northwest behind the cabin. Faint at times, it passes under two large logs and eventually arrives at a lengthy, steep slope of talus and boulders on your left (west). Some easy hand work is needed to ascend this slope. After the rocks, proceed up and southwest through more trees and over a talus slope. The trail reaches timberline at the same point as the first trail. Be sure to keep left of the rocky crag.

By either route, it is about a 90 minute hike from the Buffalo Cabin to this spot and another thirty minutes over tundra and talus to the top. The summit is on the right (north) side of a ridge and it has a small cairn. (Some hand work will be necessary if you wish to traverse to a subpeak at the south end of the ridge for views of the valley.) Descend via the first route mentioned, picking up a clear trail from where the bushes begin below the talus and tundra.

69 Peak 8 12,987 Feet

DISTANCE: 4.4 miles each way

STARTING ELEVATION: 11,000 feet

ELEVATION GAIN: 2,287 feet (includes 150 feet extra each way)

HIKING TIME: Up in 160 minutes, down in 115 minutes

TRAIL: Initial 3.6 miles, off-trail tundra and talus beyond

SEASON: Mid-June to early October

MAPS: Trails Illustrated #109

NEAREST LANDMARK: Breckenridge

GETTING THERE: From Ski Hill Road in Breckenridge, drive south on CO-9 for 2.2 miles and turn right onto Crown Road. Follow Crown Road for 0.5 mile and take a right fork, joining Spruce Creek Road. Keep straight on Spruce Creek Road, past several side roads, for 1.4 miles from the Crown Road fork, keeping

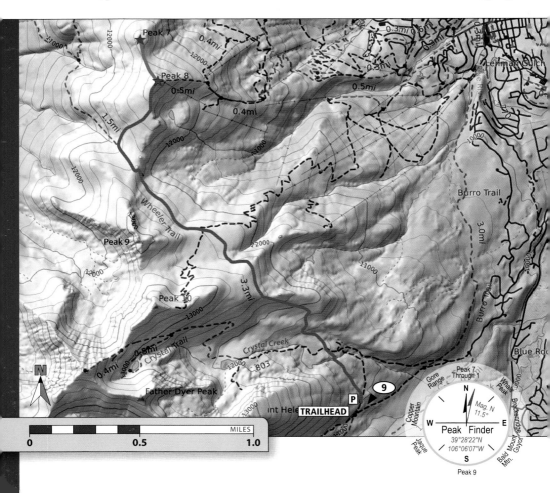

left at a fork and sign. (The right fork leads to Lower Crystal Lake.) Continue up the left fork for another 0.5 mile to a junction with the Wheeler Trail at a sign. Turn right (north) and ascend the road for 50 yards and park near a road barrier. Regular cars with good clearance can reach this point.

COMMENTS: The eastern slopes of Peak 8 and 9 are part of the Breckenridge Ski Area. Breckenridge was named after President Buchanan's Vice President, John Cabell Breckinridge of Kentucky. When he became a Confederate general, Union supporters in the area agitated to change the first "i" to an "e".

This hike is mostly above timberline with wonderful views all around. From the top, Copper Mountain, Breckenridge and Lake Dillon can all be seen. Summer wildflowers are everywhere on this high alpine hike into the heart of the Tenmile Range.

Peak 8 from the Wheeler Trail saddle.

THE ROUTE: Head up the road for 35 yards, then northwest on the Wheeler Trail, up and over logs at Crystal Creek. Ascend a ridge, continuing northwest (straight at a four-way junction) and traverse the eastern flanks of Peaks 10 and 9, en route to a saddle between Peaks 8 and 9. The trail continues west and north from this saddle down to Copper Mountain. However, leave the trail at the saddle and proceed north up a ridge for 0.8 mile to a cairn at the summit. Descend via the same route.

(From the Peak 8 summit, it is only 0.45 mile north and mostly downhill to the lower Peak 7, with no special danger or difficulty, if you wish to extend your outing. However, you will have to regain nearly 400 feet on your return back over Peak 8.)

70 North Twin Cone Peak 12,319 Feet
Mount Blaine 12,303 Feet

DISTANCE: 4.5 miles each way

STARTING ELEVATION: 10,050 feet

ELEVATION GAIN: 2,489 feet (includes 110 extra feet each way)

HIKING TIME: Up to N. Twin Cone in 149 minutes, from N. Twin Cone to Mount Blaine
in 32 minutes, down in 128 minutes

TRAIL: Initial 2.6 miles, with some off-trail walking on tundra

SEASON: Early June to early October

MAPS: Trails Illustrated#105

NEAREST LANDMARK: Jefferson

GETTING THERE: From Kenosha Pass on US-285, between Jefferson to the south and Bailey to the north, drive east on a wide, dirt road. After 0.2 mile, go right at a four-way intersection (toilets on the left). Then follow a bumpy, main road

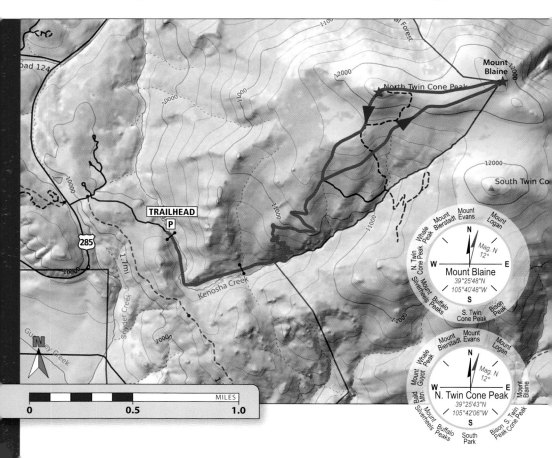

for 0.8 mile to a locked gate. Park nearby and don't block the road. If the gate is unlocked, high clearance and four-wheel drive vehicles can continue up this road for several more miles.

COMMENTS: Kenosha Pass and Creek were named after Kenosha, Wisconsin, the hometown of a local stagecoach driver.

In July, the understory of the aspen forest here is filled with colorful columbine, golden banner, and larkspur. But this hike is not to be missed in September! The slopes on the east side of Kenosha Pass are ablaze with colors ranging from fire red to golden yellow, with one of the most magnificent displays of aspen in the Front Range.

THE ROUTE: Start hiking to the east around the locked gate. Follow the rough road in open terrain, past several beaver dams and a private cabin on the left. After 1.25 miles, hike around a second locked gate and continue up the main road as it rises more steeply, with several switchbacks through thick aspen groves. At mile 2.5 of the hike, keep right at a road fork and continue upward another 0.5 mile to a key point for this hike. A blue diamond marker will be on a tree to the left and a pole with an arrow on the right side of the road. The main road circuitously leads to the summit, but the shorter, more direct route will be described here.

Enter the trees to the left (southwest) on a faint trail and follow it generally north-northeast through a large clearing. Briefly rejoin the road, and then either follow it or proceed directly to the top of North Twin Cone Peak, which will be visible over the last third of your ascent. An antenna, a benchmark, and some metal remnants mark the summit.

To reach Mount Blaine, proceed east using the four-wheel drive road briefly before heading directly to the collection of large boulders at the Mount Blaine summit. To descend, head southwest and regain the four-wheel drive road, following it to just below timberline, where you pick up your ascent route.

North Twin Cone Peak viewed from near treeline.

71 Paiute Peak 13,088 Feet

DISTANCE: 4.0 miles each way

STARTING ELEVATION: 10,470 feet

ELEVATION GAIN: 2,718 feet (includes 50 extra feet each way)

HIKING TIME: Up in 165 minutes, down in 125 minutes

TRAIL: Initial 3.0 miles, tundra and talus beyond

SEASON: Mid-June to early October

MAPS: Trails Illustrated #102

NEAREST LANDMARK: Nederland

GETTING THERE: From the town of Nederland, drive west and then north on CO-72 for about 11.7 miles. Turn left (west) onto the road to Brainard Lake. Soon you will come to an entrance station where you must pay a day-use fee. After 4.9 miles on this road, keep left and cross two bridges at the edge of Brainard Lake. Take

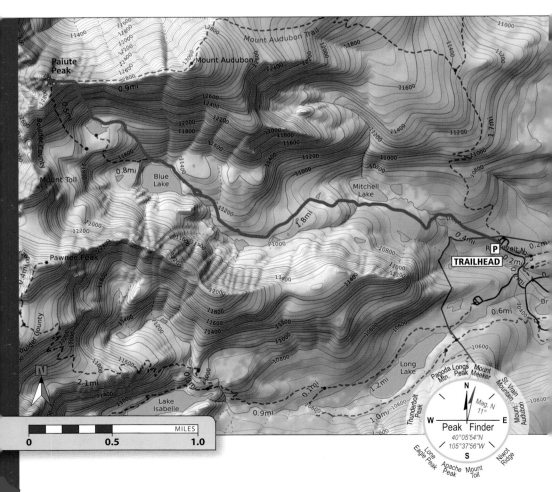

right forks at 5.35 miles, at 5.5 miles, and at 5.7 miles. Park in the lot for access to Mitchell Lake and Blue Lake, a total of 5.85 miles from CO-72. Get an early start, as the parking lots fill up quickly on weekends.

Approaching the summit of Paiute Peak. (Nelson Chenkin)

COMMENTS: The Indian Peaks Wilderness, with its pristine lakes, remnant glaciers, and rugged peaks, has long been a favorite with Front Range residents. The danger of this place being loved to death prompted the Forest Service to institute a use fee and overnight permit system.

Many of the summits, including Paiute Peak, have wonderful, evocative names that honor American Indian tribes that lived in the shadow of the Rockies, a suggestion pushed by Ellsworth Bethel in the 1920s. Paiute Peak, tucked away behind the bulk of Mount Audubon, has a wilder, less-crowded feel than the other summits in this popular playground.

THE ROUTE: Take the trail leading west. It begins to the left of a wooden sign and map. Soon a bridge crosses a creek. Later you will cross another creek over logs, with Mitchell Lake after 0.7 mile. Follow the clear trail for another 1.7 miles to nearby Blue Lake, with Mount Toll looming impressively to the west. Continue on the trail as it curves to the right around the lake and continues upward to the west, ending near a smaller lake. Leave this lake and ascend to your right (northwest) over boulders. Then continue up a moderately steep gulch to the northwest. The footing is loose at times as you ascend to a saddle and then north to a flat summit. A boulder with a pile of rocks and a makeshift register mark the highpoint. Avoid the temptation to descend to the east toward Mount Audubon (unless you wish to hike to that summit), and instead, return more securely by your ascent route.

WILD.
AREA

CMC
CLASSIC
HIKE

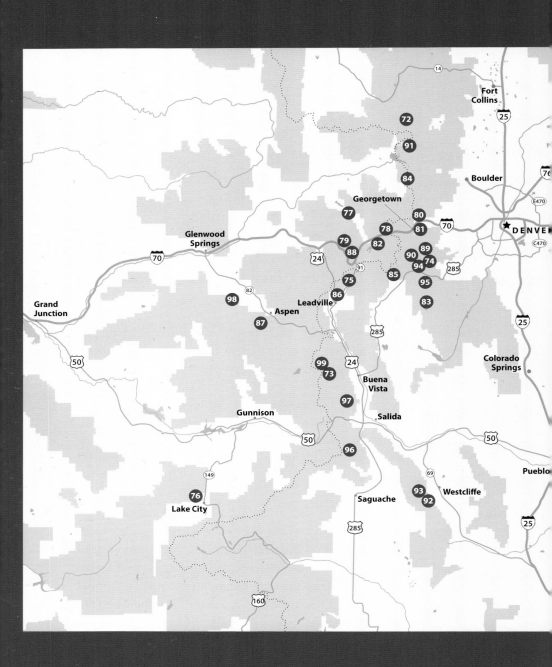

72 Mount Chiquita 13,069 Feet
Ypsilon Mountain 13,514 Feet

DISTANCE: 4.4 miles on ascent, 4.2 miles on descent

STARTING ELEVATION: 11,020 feet

ELEVATION GAIN: 3,123 feet (includes 629 extra feet)

HIKING TIME: Up to Mount Chiquita in 122 minutes, over to Ypsilon Mountain in 54 minutes, down in 106 minutes

TRAIL: All the way to Mount Chiquita, intermittent thereafter

SEASON: July to October

MAPS: Trails Illustrated #200

NEAREST LANDMARK: Estes Park

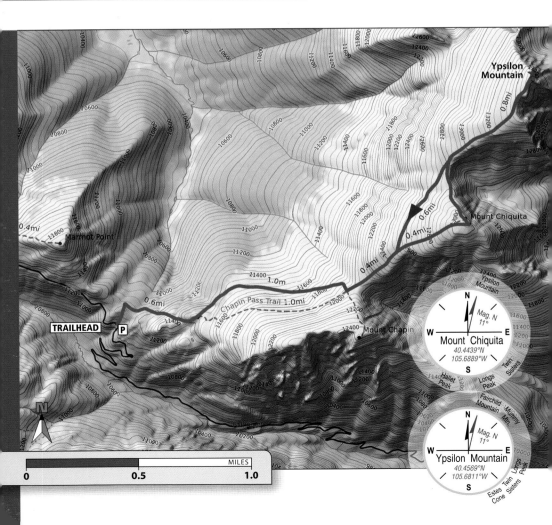

Ypsilon Mountain.

COMMENTS: Mount Chiquita and Ypsilon Mountain are part of the Mummy Range in Rocky Mountain National Park. Climbing them is comfortable with a largely gradual ascent. The drop-offs to the east of these peaks are very steep. A park ranger was killed in a fall on the east side of Ypsilon Mountain in 2005. Ypsilon is a Greek letter that resembles a snow pattern on the mountain's east face.

GETTING THERE: From the Fall River entrance to Rocky Mountain National Park west of Estes Park, drive 2.0 miles on US-34 to Horseshoe Park. Then turn right, avoid the parking areas on the right and continue up Fall River Road, which is one-way going up. Keep right at mile 3.8 from US-34 and park along the left side of the road at mile 10.4, which is near the Chapin Pass trailhead on the right. Regular cars can negotiate Fall River Road.

THE ROUTE: Start out north-northeast and after a steep 100 yards, reach a signed fork at Chapin Pass. Proceed to the right and soon take a left fork toward a saddle south of Mount Chiquita. Continue up the left to the Chiquita summit.

For Ypsilon Mountain, descend north to a saddle. Then continue up to the north over intermittent trail and past a false summit to a rock pile on top the Ypsilon summit. Enjoy the views, refresh, and on the return descend to the saddle between Chiquita and Ypsilon and try to stay level as you pass along the flanks of Mount Chiquita on the left and reach the ascent trail back to your starting point. If you still have some pep in your step, pop on over to Mount Chapin too.

73 Birthday Peak 12,730 Feet

DISTANCE: 4.6 miles each way

STARTING ELEVATION: 9,840 feet

ELEVATION GAIN: 2,890 feet

HIKING TIME: Up in 153 minutes, down in 107 minutes

TRAIL: Initial 1.8 miles, intermittent trail beyond

SEASON: Mid-June to early October

MAPS: Trails Illustrated #129

NEAREST LANDMARK: Buena Vista

GETTING THERE: Drive north on US-24 from the only stoplight in Buena Vista for 0.4 mile, or drive south on US-24 from the intersection with CO-82 for 19.3 miles. Turn west onto Crossman Avenue, which is also Chaffee County Road 350. Drive 2.1 miles to a "T" and turn right on Chaffee County Road 361. After 0.9 mile, turn sharply left onto Chaffee County Road 365 at the sign, "North Cottonwood

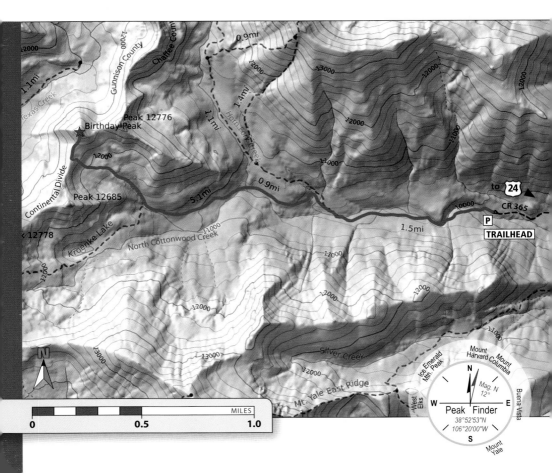

Creek 4 miles." Stay on this road for 5.3 miles, as it goes west and up into the valley, to a road end and a parking area. A sign alongside the trail reads: "North Cottonwood Creek Trail, Bear Lake 5 miles, Kroenke Lake 4 miles, Browns Pass 6 miles."

Birthday Peak.

COMMENTS: This mountain forms part of the Continental Divide and lies on the boundary between Chaffee and Gunnison Counties. The trail that is used for the initial part of this hike continues to Kroenke Lake, Browns Pass, and over to Cottonwood Pass Road. Birthday Peak is in a section of the Sawatch Range known as the Collegiate Peaks for its impressive collection of skyscraping fourteeners, with names like Harvard, Columbia, Yale, and Princeton.

THE ROUTE: Proceed west up into the basin on the clear trail and cross two wooden bridges. At about 1.8 miles from the trailhead there is a fork. Keep left and continue toward Kroenke Lake. (The right turn goes to spectacular Horn Fork Basin at the foot of Mount Harvard and Mount Columbia.) After about 1.6 miles from the fork, you will reach a creek flowing toward the southeast. Just before this creek, leave the main trail and hike northwest, up along the creek. A faint trail is present at first, and then intermittent as you ascend. It is 0.9 mile from the main trail to the saddle left of Birthday Peak, and 0.3 mile more over tundra and talus to the top, which holds a small cairn and some scattered wooden poles and wire. Be sure to identify Birthday Peak to the northwest as you follow the creek to timberline. A slightly higher, unnamed peak lies directly to the east.

WILD. AREA

CMC CLASSIC HIKE

74 Rosedale Peak 11,825 Feet

DISTANCE: 5.1 miles each way

STARTING ELEVATION: 8,960 feet

ELEVATION GAIN: 2,865 feet

HIKING TIME: Up in 186 minutes, down in 134 minutes

TRAIL: Initial 4.0 miles, bushwhack beyond

SEASON: Late May to late October

MAPS: Pikes National Forest

NEAREST LANDMARK: Bailey

GETTING THERE: From US-285, 2.7 miles east of Bailey or 4.5 miles west of Pine Junction, turn north on Park County Road 43 and continue for 6.9 miles to a fork. Take the right turn, which is Park County Road 47. After 1.5 miles farther, a dirt road leads off left (north), with a sign indicating 1.0 mile to the trailhead for the

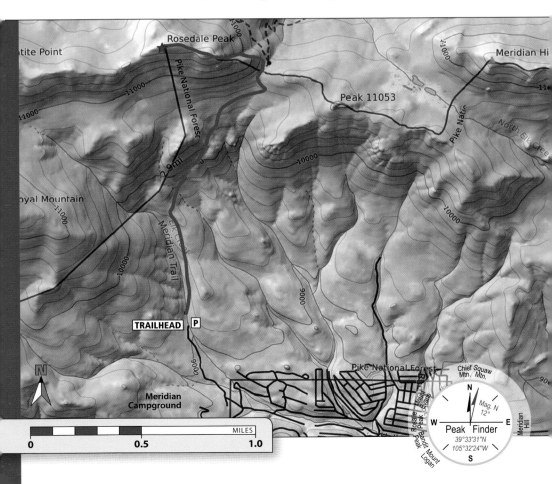

Meridian Trail. Follow this narrow road, passing Camp Rosalie after 0.3 mile. Continue on to the trailhead parking area.

COMMENTS: Rosedale Peak lies at the eastern edge of the so-called Pegmatite Points. Pegmatites are very coarse-grained, granitic rocks that typically form in dikes and isolated stocks. They have an unusual chemistry that often includes rare elements and sometimes gems such as aquamarine, garnet, and topaz. This ridge is studded with several of these odd outcrops.

The summit ridge forms part of the boundary between the Pike and Arapaho National Forests. The trail over the unnamed pass continues north, penetrating into the eastern half of the wonderful Mount Evans Wilderness.

THE ROUTE: From the signed trailhead, hike north along the Meridian Trail. After about five minutes from the trailhead, a fork is reached. The left route is Church Fork Road. Take the right fork, which is the Meridian Trail. Continue north on the trail, soon reaching a clearing and a horse corral on your left. A sign indicates that the road will dead end. The trail cuts off to the right, crosses Elk Creek by way of a small wooden bridge and then cuts left (north), gradually ascending to an unnamed, unmarked pass at 10,700 feet. Continue north on the trail about 200 yards past the pass and then bushwhack left (west), steeply up for 0.9 mile to a summit ridge and then to a summit boulder. Keep north on the ridge. The highpoint is on the west end of the ridge. There are no markers at the top. Descend by the ascent route.

WILD.
AREA

Rosedale Peak viewed from Harris Park. (Eric Wiseman)

75 Corbett Peak 12,583 Feet

DISTANCE: 4.8 miles on ascent, 3.4 miles on descent

STARTING ELEVATION: 9,560 feet

ELEVATION GAIN: 3,023 feet

HIKING TIME: Up in 190 minutes, down in 100 minutes

TRAIL: Trail to timberline, intermittent beyond

SEASON: Early June to early October

MAPS: Trails Illustrated #109

NEAREST LANDMARK: Leadville

GETTING THERE: Either drive on US-24 north from Leadville for 11.3 miles or south from Minturn for 18.8 miles. Turn northeast onto a dirt road (Road 726). After 2.9 miles the road arrives at a "T." Turn right and go 0.7 more miles and park off the road. Regular passenger cars can easily reach this point.

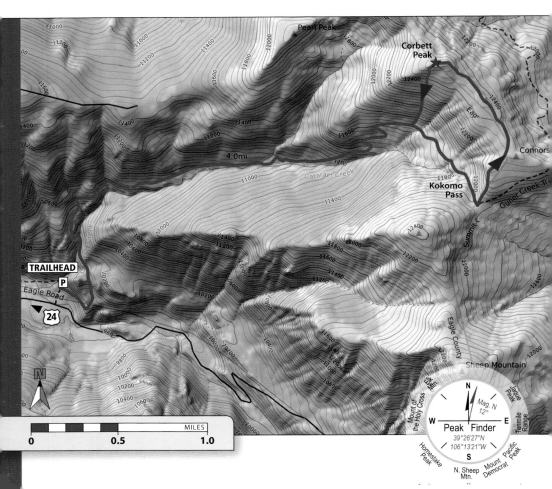

COMMENTS: Kokomo Pass lies west of Kokomo Gulch and the now-abandoned town of Kokomo. These places were named after Kokomo, Indiana, the hometown of some of the area residents. Corbett Peak lies on Elk Ridge, which divides Eagle and Summit Counties and offers excellent views of Mount of the Holy Cross to the west.

Cataract Creek leaves rolling alpine meadows filled with flowers and tumbles down a steepening gorge. The sound of falling water is always near. Since 2002, the Forest Service requires hikers to stay on the Colorado Trail along the Cataract Creek corridor because of old munitions found in the Camp Hale area. Camping or wandering off the trail are not permitted. Any munitions discovered should be reported.

THE ROUTE: The trail begins on the north side of the road at a "No Motor Vehicles" sign. Continue

Cairn just below Kokomo Pass. (Julie Mesdag)

north for about 180 yards to a fork, where the Colorado Trail is intercepted. Turn right (east) onto the trail, an old logging road that climbs rather steeply to an abandoned cabin and sawmill, crosses Cataract Creek and generally proceeds to the east. After some switchbacks just before timberline, the creek is crossed again and the trail passes through lovely alpine meadows, before a final short, steep ravine to Kokomo Pass at 12,022 feet, the low point on the ridge to the east. From the unmarked pass, leave the Colorado Trail, following the ridge trail north, and then northwest, to gain the rocky outcroppings at the unmarked top of Corbett Peak.

Descend over the tundra to the southwest, rejoin the trail of your ascent route just below timberline, and follow it west and southwest back to the trailhead.

76 Matterhorn Peak 13,590 Feet

DISTANCE: 4.5 miles each way

STARTING ELEVATION: 10,390 feet

ELEVATION GAIN: 3,200 feet

HIKING TIME: Up in 143 minutes, down in 103 minutes

TRAIL: Initial 3.6 miles, mostly tundra and talus beyond and a trail near the summit

SEASON: Mid-June to early October

MAPS: Trails Illustrated #141

NEAREST LANDMARK: Lake City

GETTING THERE: From CO-149 in Lake City, drive west on Second Avenue, just north of the Henson Creek Bridge. This road quickly turns left (south) and then follows Henson Creek to the west. It eventually leads over Engineer Pass to Ouray and Silverton, but you will not go that far. Instead, drive 9.3 miles from CO-149

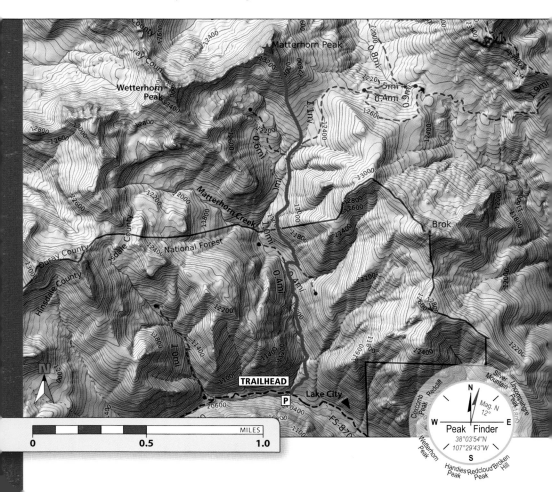

Matterhorn Peak viewed from the south.

to a fork at the old site of Capitol City. Turn right (northwest) up the North Fork of Henson Creek for 2.0 miles. Park around Matterhorn Creek and a road leading north and up the creek. Regular cars can come this far, but four-wheel drive is required for the 0.7 mile north up Matterhorn Creek, where the road is blocked.

COMMENTS: This hike requires less elevation gain, route finding, rock work, and risk than nearby Wetterhorn Peak. In naming these two peaks after their Swiss counterparts, the names seemingly should have been reversed, since in Switzerland, the Matterhorn is the higher, more dramatic summit.

The immense hulk of Uncompahgre Peak, sixth highest peak in Colorado, sits to the east. These peaks are remnants of volcanic activity in the San Juan Mountains, with Wetterhorn Peak believed to be an ancient plug.

THE ROUTE: Hike up this rough road to the north, marked by a sign, "Ridge Stock Driveway Trail." This road keeps to the right of Matterhorn Creek and is quite steep to above timberline. In half an hour, you will reach the vehicle barricade, and in another 30 minutes, you pass a wilderness sign (The Big Blue Wilderness). Follow the road as it passes timberline, curves northeast away from the creek, and then north again. Matterhorn Peak lies directly ahead. Do not confuse it with the taller Wetterhorn Peak to the left (west). When you can see a direct route up Matterhorn's southeast ridge, without losing any elevation, leave the road and proceed northwest, up over steep tundra. When the tundra ends and the rocks begin, a trail emerges and continues up an easily negotiated couloir to the unmarked summit rock pile. Descend by your ascent route.

WILD.
AREA

CMC
CLASSIC
HIKE

77 Bills Peak 12,703 Feet

DISTANCE: 4.8 miles each way

STARTING ELEVATION: 9,708 feet

ELEVATION GAIN: 3,195 feet (includes 100 feet extra each way)

HIKING TIME: Up in 151 minutes, down in 110 minutes

TRAIL: Most of the way, with off-trail tundra near the top

SEASON: Mid-June to early October

MAPS: Trails Illustrated #103

NEAREST LANDMARK: Silverthorne

GETTING THERE: From the Dillon and Silverthorne area at the intersection of I-70 and CO-9, drive north on CO-9 for 12.8 miles. Turn right (east) on Summit County Road 15, also known as Ute Pass Road. After 5.4 miles on this paved road, cross Ute Pass. In 2.2 more miles, take the left fork and bypass the Henderson

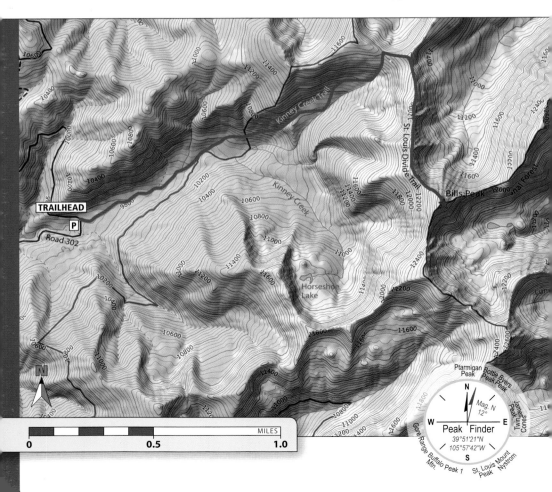

Mine. Keep left after 0.7 mile, and in 0.9 more miles, turn right at a sign onto Grand County Road 30. Follow this good road for 2.6 miles, turning left (east) onto Grand County Road 302 and at a sign directing you east to the Kinney Creek Trail. After 3.6 miles on this road, at a bend in the road just past Kinney Creek, is the well-marked trailhead. Park here off the road.

Bills (center) and Byers Peaks.

COMMENTS: The trail for this hike is clear and exceptionally well marked. Bills Peak is the second highest mountain in the Byers Peak Wilderness. From the summit, you are rewarded with panoramic views of a relatively remote region.

THE ROUTE: Proceed east at the trail sign and register. Kinney Creek remains on your right as you ascend the valley. In 50 minutes, you reach a fork and a sign. The right fork leads to Horseshoe Lake in 2.5 miles. Take the left fork, which leads to Evelyn Lake and the St. Louis Divide Trail. In another 44 minutes, you will arrive at a saddle and a sign, having passed several poles in cairns. The sign points left to the Keyser Ridge Road (2 miles) and right to the Keyser Creek Road (2 miles) and to St. Louis Lake (4 miles). Turn right (east) and follow the trail past timberline. At a ridge, turn right (south) and pick up the trail that continues along the west side of the ridge. In about 54 minutes from the saddle, leave the trail at a cairn and ascend steeply east to the summit, which has an erroneous elevation sign in a cairn. Return by your ascent route.

WILD. AREA

78 Engelmann Peak 13,362 Feet
Robeson Peak 13,140 Feet

DISTANCE: 2.15 miles to Engelmann Peak, 0.9 mile from Engelmann Peak to
Robeson Peak, 3.2 miles on return

STARTING ELEVATION: 10,000 feet

ELEVATION GAIN: 3,702 feet (includes 340 ft. extra between summits)

HIKING TIME: Up in 180 minutes, down in 95 minutes

TRAIL: Mostly bushwhacking, with 1 mile of trail on ascent and 1.75 miles on descent

SEASON: Mid-June to early October

MAPS: Trails Illustrated #103 & 104

NEAREST LANDMARK: Empire

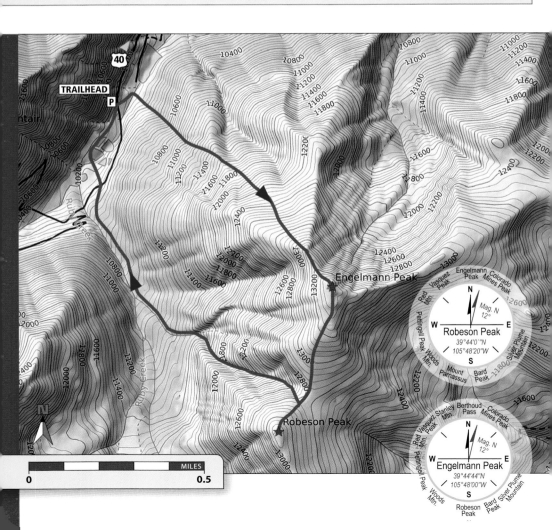

Englemann Peak viewed from the north. (Eric Wiseman)

COMMENTS: The higher peak is named after George Engelmann, a botanist and physician from St. Louis. The Engelmann spruce is also named in his honor. The lower peak is named after the well-known mining family of Georgetown. Solomon Robeson discovered many mines in Clear Creek County and his son, Jacob H. Robeson, was superintendent of the Dives Pelican Mine and mayor of Georgetown in 1898.

The impressive bulk of Engelmann Peak is a familiar sight along US-40, with a reputation for spewing deadly avalanches onto the highway in winter. Perhaps that is why few venture up its steep slopes. You are likely to have these summits to yourself. The hike is best done in September, when the creek along the descent will be at its lowest level.

GETTING THERE: On US-40, drive 7.4 miles west from Main Street in Empire toward Berthoud Pass or drive 5.9 miles south of Berthoud Pass. Turn west at the bend in the road, toward the Henderson Mine. Pass the Big Bend Picnic Ground. After 0.4 mile from US-40, take the left fork toward Urad Lake. After 0.5 mile on the wide, dirt Woods Creek Road, park near a large sign that forbids any stopping on the road for the next 3 miles.

THE ROUTE: Begin south and follow Woods Creek Road up the left side of the valley. After 0.8 mile leave the main road and ascend left on a blocked road for vehicles with an avalanche warning. Follow the road as far as you can and then head for the saddle between the two peaks. Follow the ridge up left to the Engelmann summit. Then go south over tundra down to the saddle and then up to Robeson Peak. To return, either retrace your route or go more directly down to Woods Creek Road.

79 Red Benchmark Mountain 11,816 Feet

DISTANCE: 5.1 miles each way

STARTING ELEVATION: 8,786 feet

ELEVATION GAIN: 3,240 feet (includes 210 feet extra each way)

HIKING TIME: Up in 160 minutes, down in 105 minutes

TRAIL: All the way

SEASON: Mid-June to early October

MAPS: Trails Illustrated #108

NEAREST LANDMARK: East Vail

GETTING THERE: From I-70 in East Vail, take Exit 201 and drive 2.5 miles on Bighorn Road, which runs along the south side of the Interstate. Park near the road barrier, as the former US-6 continues up toward Vail Pass as a bicycle and hiking route.

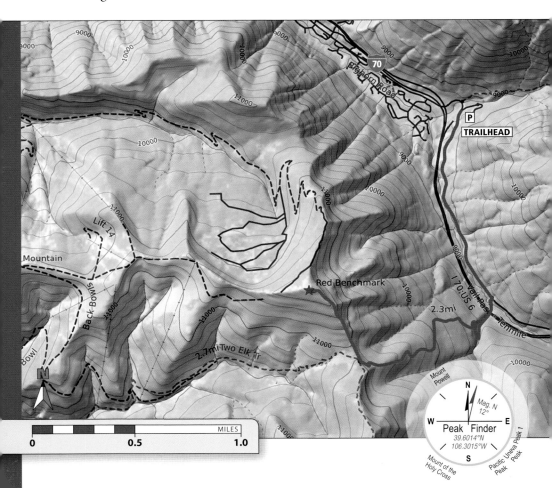

COMMENTS: This hike uses the Two Elk Trail, which runs from Vail to Minturn and is a National Scenic Trail. The red sandstone formations and the cascading water as the trail passes under I-70 add much to the route.

THE ROUTE: Begin south up the road from the barrier. After 1.8 miles, leave the road at a sign and descend to a bridge crossing Gore Creek. Hike under the highway and after 2.0 steep miles, reach Two Elk Pass at a fork. Bowmans Shortcut goes left but you go to the right. After 0.25 mile from the pass, take a right fork and ascend north-northwest another 1.0 mile to markers at the top of Red Benchmark Mountain. Enjoy your high perch before your return to the trailhead.

After a thunderstorm.

80 Breckinridge Peak 12,889 Feet

DISTANCE: 5.1 miles each way

STARTING ELEVATION: 9,800 feet

ELEVATION GAIN: 3,419 feet (includes 165 feet extra each way)

HIKING TIME: Up in 165 minutes, down in 110 minutes

TRAIL: Initial 4.0 miles, bushwhack beyond

SEASON: Mid-June to early October

MAPS: Trails Illustrated #103

NEAREST LANDMARK: Empire

GETTING THERE: From the center of Empire on US-40, drive north on Main Street. Take right forks at 0.7, 1.1, 1.6, 1.8, and 1.9 miles. Stay on the main road, which is rough and a bit steep in spots toward the end. Park at mile 2.3 from US-40 at the former Conqueror Mine.

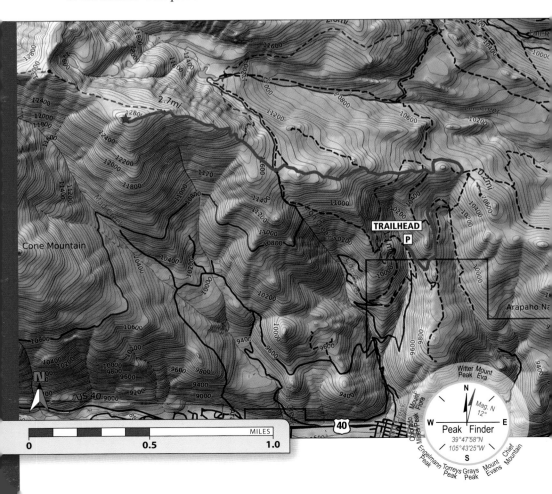

Breckinridge Peak from the southeast.

COMMENTS: The Conqueror group of mines numbered over ten and were begun in 1881 to mine gold and silver. After closing down, they reopened again in 1901. The striking, abandoned mine building north of the trailhead was part of this complex.

The peak maintains the original spelling of President Buchanan's Vice President, John Cabell Breckinridge. Named by E.H.N. Patterson on October 4, 1860, this is actually a subpeak of Mount Flora to the west. Mount Flora, in turn, was named by Dr. Charles Parry, who explored this group of peaks on the east side of Berthoud Pass in 1861, and as a botanist, was charmed by the great profusion of miniature alpine plants. A hike along this ridge in June is still a delightful experience with alpine forget-me-nots, mountain avens, and old-man-of-the-mountain to charm the senses.

WILD.
AREA

THE ROUTE: Begin southwest on the road, which soon becomes rougher. Stay on the main road and avoid side roads to the left at mile 0.1, 0.2 and 0.3. The road then curves left. Keep straight at a four-way intersection at mile 0.6, then 100 yards farther, go right. Take another right fork in 0.2 more miles and within 100 yards farther, take the first of five consecutive left forks over the next mile. The last of these leads steeply north-northwest to a "T." Go left, make a quick right fork and ascend to a ridge. Keep west on the ridge and take two more left forks before arriving at the foot of Breckinridge Peak. Leave the road and ascend west-northwest up the ridge for another 1.5 miles to a cairn at the summit. You will cross a segment of the Continental Divide Trail that traverses this ridge, passing close by the summit. Return by retracing your ascent route. Be careful to take the correct trail forks.

81 Republican Mountain 12,386 Feet

DISTANCE: 5.6 miles each way

STARTING ELEVATION: 9,000 feet

ELEVATION GAIN: 3,506 feet

HIKING TIME: Up in 157 minutes, down in 106 minutes

TRAIL: Most of the way to timberline, easy tundra walking beyond

SEASON: Mid-June to early October

MAPS: Trails Illustrated #104

NEAREST LANDMARK: Empire

GETTING THERE: Drive south from Empire on Bard Creek Road as it cuts off US-40 from the center of town. Continue on this road for 2.0 miles as it curves west past Empire Pass, overlooking I-70, until reaching a rough road on your left. Park here. A regular car can come this far. Difficult four-wheel driving would be required beyond this point toward Republican Mountain.

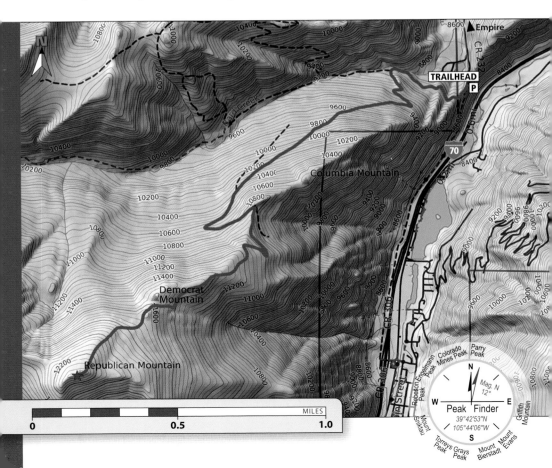

COMMENTS: The route up Republican Mountain should be free of snow between June and October. Four nearby fourteeners can be seen from the top—Grays Peak, Torreys Peak, Mount Evans, and Mount Bierstadt. Approaching the summit, be on the lookout for bighorn sheep, often spotted along the top of this ridge in the summer. They are part of the large Georgetown herd that winters on the lower, south-facing slopes between Idaho Springs and Georgetown and are often seen by I-70 motorists. This successful herd is often trapped for restocking operations around the state.

The names of Republican Mountain and others along this ridge are of Civil War vintage and reflect the political loyalties of the day.

Republican Mountain from treeline.

THE ROUTE: Start your hike going south up the rough side road. After a few hundred yards, take a left fork and stay on the main ascending road. After several curves in the road and after passing several mining ruins, you will arrive at the high point of the road, 4.5 miles from the trailhead. The top of Republican Mountain will now be visible ahead. The road continues down and east through Silver Gulch toward Georgetown. But leave the road and its highpoint, angling up and west about a hundred yards through the sparse trees to the ridge. Then ascend west-southwest along the ridge over the tundra to the rocky summit. Keep to the right of any residual snow. A benchmark and a pole mark the mountaintop. Enjoy the sights before retracing the lengthy ascent route.

82

Grays Peak 14,270 Feet
Torreys Peak 14,267 Feet

DISTANCE: 4.3 miles to Grays Peak, 0.7 mile from Grays Peak to Torreys Peak,
4.5 miles on return

STARTING ELEVATION: 11,230 feet

ELEVATION GAIN: 3,944 feet (includes 894 ft. extra between summits)

HIKING TIME: Up Grays Peak in 135 minutes, Grays Peak to Torreys Peak in 35 minutes,
down in 90 minutes

TRAIL: All the way

SEASON: Late June to early October

MAPS: Trails Illustrated #104

NEAREST LANDMARK: Bakerville

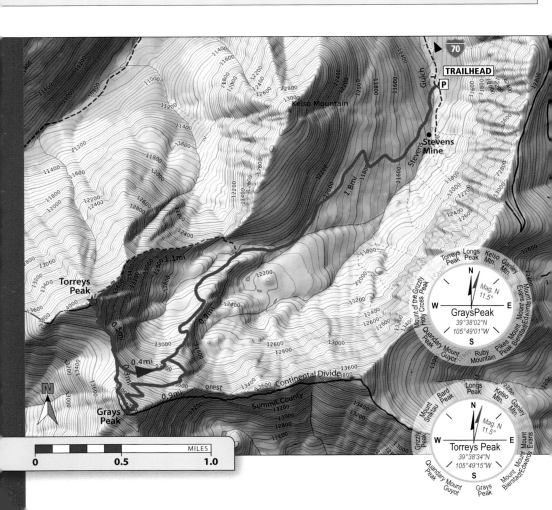

GETTING THERE: Drive south from the Bakerville exit (Exit # 221) off I-70 for 3.4 miles to the trailhead. The road is blocked just before the defunct Stevens Mine, farther south. En route to the parking area near the trailhead, take left forks at mile 1.35 and mile 2.3. A regular car can make it up this steep, rough road to the trailhead area. Restrooms and an information board are next to the large, gravel parking area. On summer weekends, the parking lot fills up very early with hikers intent on climbing the twin fourteeners. Late arrivals may be forced to park alongside the access road.

COMMENTS: These peaks were named after the famous botanists, Asa Gray and John Torrey by colleague Charles C. Parry. They are considered two of the easier fourteeners to climb. Oddly enough, they are the only fourteeners that lie on the Continental Divide.

Grays (left) and Torreys Peaks viewed from Mount Kelso.

These are very popular hikes due to their proximity to Denver. A herd of mountain goats are often present near the trail, seemingly oblivious to a steady stream of climbers.

THE ROUTE: Hike southwest over the bridge. Follow the wide trail up past timberline, with Kelso Mountain on the right. After 1.25 miles from the trailhead, cross the creek. The top of Grays Peak and the trail are plainly visible to the south from here. Near the summit, there are several connecting trails that all lead to the top. The final thousand feet of elevation is over a talus trail, reaching a rock shelter at the highpoint.

To continue over to Torreys Peak, descend northwest on a faint trail to the saddle. Then ascend the ridge, over talus, to a rock pile atop Torreys Peak. Enjoy the views.

Descend to the saddle and continue 50 feet up toward Grays Peak, before turning left on a trail and cutting back across the face to the Grays Peak Trail. This segment is snow-covered most of the hiking season. Early in the season, many people choose to glissade back down into the basin.

83 Bison Peak 12,431 Feet

DISTANCE: 6.7 miles on ascent, 4.1 miles on descent

STARTING ELEVATION: 9,910 feet

ELEVATION GAIN: 2,521 feet

HIKING TIME: Up in 180 minutes, down in 105 minutes

TRAIL: Most of the way, with some bushwhacking

SEASON: Early June to early October

MAPS: Trails Illustrated #105

NEAREST LANDMARK: Jefferson

GETTING THERE: Drive on US-285 for 3.2 miles south of Kenosha Pass and turn east onto a good dirt road marked by a sign, "Lost Creek Road." (This road lies just north of the town of Jefferson.) Stay on this main dirt road going east-southeast for 19.7 miles and park. This trailhead is just west of the Lost Park Campground. Regular passenger cars should have no trouble.

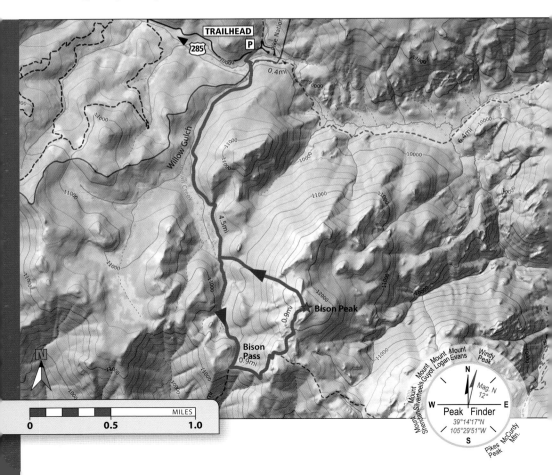

Bison Peak (left) viewed from the southwest.

COMMENTS: Bison Peak is the highest in the Tarryall Range. The name Tarryall is said to have originated when miners found such abundant gold in this area that they believed there was enough for all (Tarry-all). McCurdy Mountain is an easy tundra walk of 2.0 miles along the McCurdy Park Trail to the southeast, if you have the time and the energy.

This hike enters the Lost Creek Wilderness, with its fascinating domes and knobs of pink Pikes Peak granite. Lost Creek gets its name from its habit of disappearing into piles of rock, only to reappear farther downstream. Be on a sharp lookout for bighorn sheep, very common around Bison Peak.

THE ROUTE: Cross to the south side of the creek, where there are some signs and a trail passing east-west. Take the trail going south, called the Indian Creek Trail # 607, passing up into the trees at a clearing. Follow this trail south into Willow Gulch, eventually reaching a large open valley. After about 4.7 miles, the Indian Creek Trail reaches Bison Pass at 11,100 feet. Here lies a three-way trail intersection. Signs direct you to Tarryall Creek 4 miles to the south; to Lost Creek 5.25 miles north (the route you have just taken); and McCurdy Park 5.75 miles to the east. Follow the McCurdy Park Trail up and to the east to above timberline, where numerous and impressive red granite formations are encountered. As the trail turns south, leave it and head northeast to Bison Peak and its clearly visible rocky summit. Avoid the labyrinth of boulders lying to the south of the peak and reach the unambiguous summit, where the ruins of an old platform, a stone stove, and a register jar can be found.

For the descent, hike northwest on the ridge tundra and pick your way down. Bushwhack mostly to the northwest to regain the Indian Creek Trail in the large open valley visible below. Then continue north, retracing your ascent route back to your car.

WILD. AREA

CMC CLASSIC HIKE

84 Satanta Peak 11,979 Feet
Mount Neva 12,814 Feet

DISTANCE: 2.8 miles to Arapaho Pass, 1.3 miles from Arapaho Pass to Satanta Peak,
1.25 miles from Arapaho Pass to Mt. Neva; 4.5 miles from Mt. Neva to trailhead

STARTING ELEVATION: 10,180 feet

ELEVATION GAIN: 3,157 feet for both peaks (includes 225 feet extra)

HIKING TIME: Up to Arapaho Pass 93 minutes, Arapaho Pass to Satanta Peak in 26 minutes,
back to Arapaho Pass in 26 minutes, Arapaho Pass to Mount Neva in
88 minutes, down from Mount Neva in 130 minutes.

TRAIL: Most of the way, with some scrambling on final ridges

SEASON: Early June to early October

MAPS: Trails Illustrated #102

NEAREST LANDMARK: Eldora

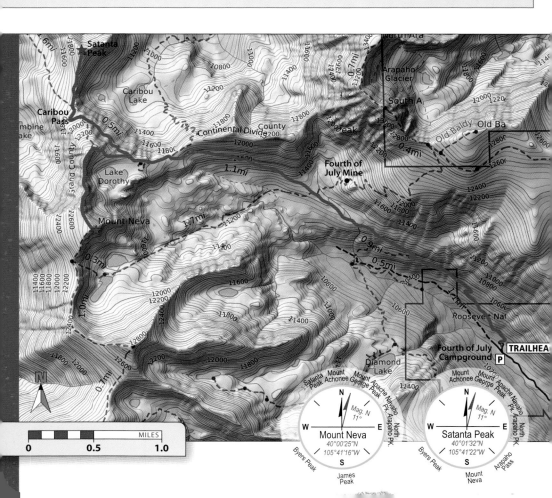

GETTING THERE: From the junction of CO-72 and CO-119 in Nederland, drive south on CO-119 for 0.65 mile and turn right (west). Drive a total of 9.1 miles from CO-119 on this road, through the town of Eldora, to a parking area at the trailhead at the Fourth of July Campground. En route keep right at 1.5 miles and at 4.9 miles. Keep left at 7.7 miles and then right to the parking area at 9.0 miles. This road, rough in a few spots after a rain, is normally suitable for a regular car.

Satanta Peak from Arapaho Pass.

COMMENTS: Arapaho Pass and Mount Neva are on the Continental Divide and on the boundary between Grand and Boulder Counties and the Roosevelt and Arapaho National Forests. This hike lies in the very popular Indian Peaks Wilderness Area.

The sunny, south-facing slopes leading up to Arapaho Pass are a riot of colors in July, with one of the finest displays of alpine wildflowers in the Front Range.

THE ROUTE: Proceed north and then west from the clearly marked trailhead. Take a right fork after 27 minutes (the left fork goes to Diamond Lake) and a left fork after 24 more minutes (the right fork goes to Arapaho Glacier and the Arapaho Peaks). Continue west above timberline on the excellent trail, which now consists of mostly flat talus, to Arapaho Pass, just northeast of Lake Dorothy. For Satanta Peak, continue southwest to the vicinity of Lake Dorothy and then descend west, contouring around the north ridge of Mount Neva. The trail becomes a bit narrow at times, but is adequate. In 13 minutes, the trail brings you to a sign marking Caribou Pass. A trail leads northwest from the pass and the Caribou Pass Trail. Follow this trail for only a few hundred feet and then leave the trail, ascending north over tundra to a large cairn atop Satanta Peak. Return to Arapaho Pass by the same route.

For Mount Neva, continue west up the north ridge on a faint trail from the area of Lake Dorothy. Follow the ridge as it turns south. At a few points along this

WILD.
AREA

CMC
CLASSIC
HIKE

ridge, some moderate hand work is necessary. Continue south and eventually reach a grassy area, leading to a cairn at the summit. Return to Arapaho Pass and the trailhead by your ascent route. (For an alternate descent route from Mount Neva, go south along the Divide to a saddle and then descend east into the basin toward Diamond Lake, where you find a trail leading east back to the Arapaho Pass Trail.)

Mount Neva.

85 Mount Guyot 13,370 Feet

DISTANCE: 5.25 miles on ascent, 2.4 miles on descent

STARTING ELEVATION: 10,390 feet

ELEVATION GAIN: 3,164 feet (includes 75 feet extra each way)

HIKING TIME: Up in 212 minutes, down in 122 minutes

TRAIL: All the way on ascent, final 0.8 mile on descent

SEASON: Mid-June to early October

MAPS: Trails Illustrated #109

NEAREST LANDMARK: Breckenridge

GETTING THERE: Drive 0.8 mile north on CO-9 from a stop light in Breckenridge at Lincoln Street. Turn right (east) onto Summit County Road 450 and drive generally south up French Gulch for 4.65 miles and park off the road at a locked

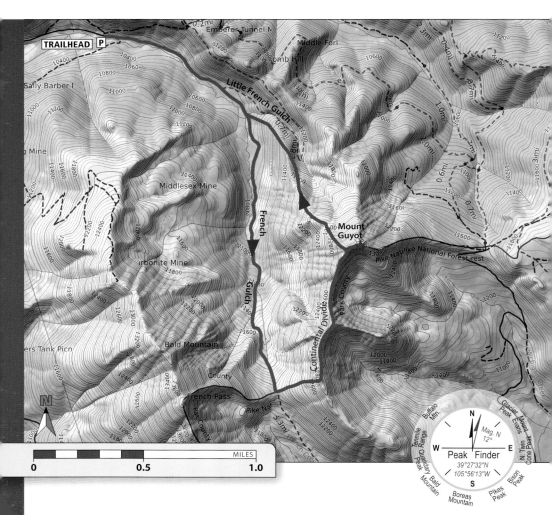

gate. En route to this parking spot from CO-9, keep right at mile 0.4, left at mile 1.1, straight at mile 3.9, left at mile 4.0, and left at mile 4.55. Regular passenger cars can reach this point.

COMMENTS: Mount Guyot is named after the Swiss surveyor, Professor Arnold Henry Guyot. Climbers, when perched on other summits, love to pick out this big, impressive peak. The huge, handsome cirque on the east face can be seen for miles around.

Mount Guyot and French Pass also form part of the Continental Divide, the boundary between Summit and Park Counties and also between the Arapaho and Pike National Forests. Mount Guyot also can be easily climbed from Georgia Pass on the east.

Mount Guyot viewed from the south.

THE ROUTE: Proceed south around the gate and avoid two roads on the left after 0.5 mile. (The second trail on the left ascends Little French Gulch.) Pass through an open meadow and enter the forest as the road steepens. At mile 2.3, reach a meaningless fork, as both roads quickly converge at another locked gate. Pass around the gate and soon cross a creek. It is 1.2 miles farther, mostly over tundra, to a cairn at French Pass. Bald Mountain is on your right (west) and Boreas Mountain lies straight ahead (south). From the pass, ascend a faint trail to the left (east-northeast), following it along the western slopes of the ridge (the Continental Divide). This trail eventually turns to the northeast to gain the cairn-marked summit. A register cylinder and some rock shelters are also at the top.

To return, descend over talus without a trail to the northwest to a ridge separating French Gulch from Little French Gulch. Around timberline, veer to your left (northwest) and bushwhack down to the road leading back to your vehicle.

86

Buckeye Peak 12,867 Feet
Mount Zion 12,126 Feet

DISTANCE: 4.3 miles to Mount Zion, 3.1 miles from Mount Zion to Buckeye Peak, 7.4 miles return

STARTING ELEVATION: 9,961 feet

ELEVATION GAIN: 3,426 feet (includes 260 feet extra each way)

HIKING TIME: Up in 220 minutes, down in 180 minutes

TRAIL: Initial 6.6 miles, tundra walking beyond

SEASON: Early June to early October

MAPS: Trails Illustrated #109

NEAREST LANDMARK: Leadville

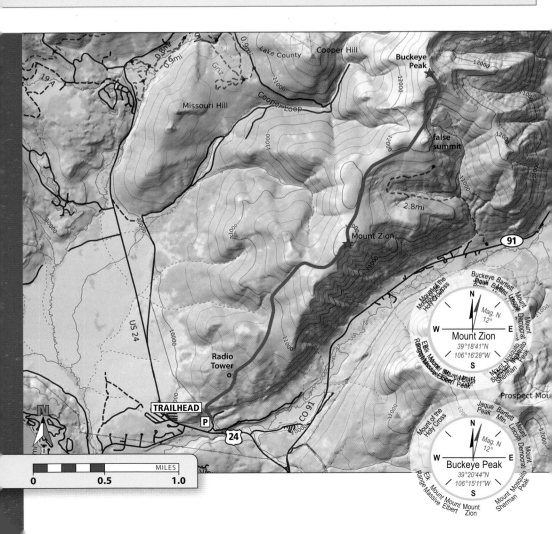

GETTING THERE: From the north end of Leadville at the intersection of CO-91 and US-24, drive northwest on US-24 for 1.4 miles. Turn right onto a dirt road at a sign stating, "Mount Zion Road 5510." In 0.1 mile, this road offers three routes. Park around here. (High-clearance and four-wheel drive vehicles can traverse the entire 6.7 miles of this road to the foot of Buckeye Peak when weather conditions permit.)

COMMENTS: Buckeye Peak was probably named by some early miners from Ohio, the Buckeye State. There are several Mount Zions in Colorado.

Despite the modest nature of these two summits, the vistas are truly exceptional. Spread out before you is a sweeping panorama of the Sawatch Range, including Mount Elbert and Mount Massive, the two

A ptarmigan resting near the summit of Buckeye Peak. (Eric Wiseman)

highest summits in the state. Beyond that is the Elk Range, with its own set of skyscraping fourteeners. Counting close-by Mounts Sherman, Lincoln, and Democrat, there are at least eighteen fourteeners visible.

With eyes drawn to these giants, don't trip over some of the many white-tailed ptarmigan in the area.

THE ROUTE: Follow the road going left (northwest), as it rises through the trees. Take the left fork at 0.25 mile and again at mile 0.8. Pass a radio tower at mile 1.3. At mile 4.3, you will be above timberline and reach Mount Zion. The summit cairn and a jar register will be a two-minute side hike off the road to the right (east). Regain the road and continue north, with some elevation loss over the rolling tundra. The jeep trail bends northeast, rising between two unnamed peaks and ending at the foot of Buckeye Peak, with little Buckeye Lake down to the right (east). Follow the rocky ridge on the right, north toward the summit, which contains three separate USGS markers and a ring of rocks around a cairn supporting a small metal tower. Return by way of your ascent route.

87 Mount Buckskin 13,370 Feet

DISTANCE: 4.5 miles each way

STARTING ELEVATION: 9,600 feet

ELEVATION GAIN: 4,170 feet (includes 200 feet extra each way)

HIKING TIME: Up in 190 minutes, down in 135 minutes

TRAIL: Initial 3.7 miles, tundra walking beyond

SEASON: Early June to early October

MAPS: Trails Illustrated #128

NEAREST LANDMARK: Aspen

GETTING THERE: The Maroon Lake area is one of the most heavily used in Colorado. The Maroon Creek Road is closed to private motor vehicles from 9:00 A.M. until 5:00 P.M. daily during the hiking season. Shuttle buses transport visitors from a parking area at the mouth of the valley for the 9 miles to Maroon Lake. Drive

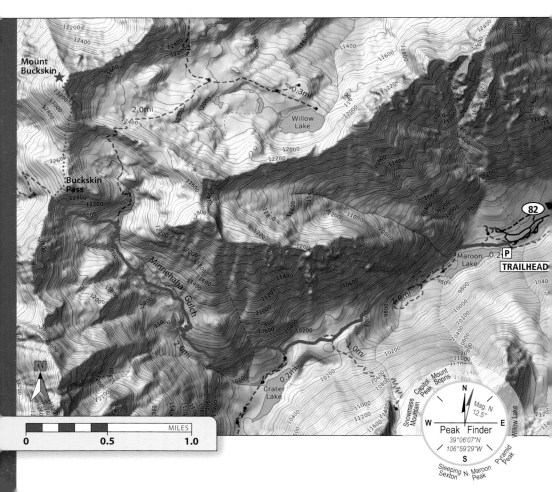

Mount Buckskin viewed from the east. (Eric Wiseman)

west on CO-82 from Aspen. Cross the Castle Creek bridge and take the first left turn after the stoplight. This turn directs you to Aspen Highlands. After 0.1 mile on this road, take the right fork to Maroon Creek. Soon you will notice the parking area for the shuttle buses. The paved road continues up the valley for a total of 9.9 miles from CO-82, until the road ends at a parking area at Maroon Lake, above the Maroon Lake Campground.

COMMENTS: This hike brings you to one of the most scenic passes in Colorado, with fantastic flower-strewn meadows to please the senses along the way. The view of the Maroon Bells, from your starting point at Maroon Lake, has to be one of the most photographed scenes in Colorado. Despite the very rugged nature of the peaks in the Elk Range, Mount Buckskin poses no special risks and offers spectacular vistas.

As of 2003, hikers are required to obtain a free permit to enter the Maroon Bells/Snowmass Wilderness, available at self-serve stations at the trailhead. There are no restrictions on the number of permits granted each day (although that could be the future for this popular area).

THE ROUTE: Take the trail, starting at the west end of the parking area at a sign stating "Maroon Snowmass Trail #1975." This leads south then turns southwest before the lake. Take two right forks en route to a sign and trail fork near Crater Lake. This fork will be reached in about 45 minutes. Take the right fork and ascend southwest into Minnehaha Gulch. In about thirty minutes from the fork at Crater Lake, take the right fork, reaching timberline in forty minutes more. About ten minutes above timberline, take the left fork at a sign (the right fork goes to Willow Pass). In another thirty minutes you will arrive, after a series of switchbacks, to unmarked, scenic Buckskin Pass. From the pass, proceed north over tundra. The Mount Buckskin summit is visible 0.8 mile from the pass. En route, you will lose about 100 feet of elevation as you pass through a saddle. Continue north over some rocky false summits to the top, which has a cairn, USGS marker, and a small register jar. Retrace the ascent route back to the trailhead.

WILD.
AREA

CMC
CLASSIC
HIKE

88 Uneva Peak 12,522 Feet

DISTANCE: 7.0 miles on ascent, 6.0 miles on descent

STARTING ELEVATION: 9,660 feet

ELEVATION GAIN: 2,902 feet (includes 40 feet extra)

HIKING TIME: Up in 210 minutes, down in 160 minutes

TRAIL: Initial 4.8 miles, tundra walking beyond

SEASON: Early June to early October

MAPS: Trails Illustrated #108

NEAREST LANDMARK: Copper Mountain

GETTING THERE: Drive west on I-70 for 4.8 miles past Exit #201 and park in the lot on the right.

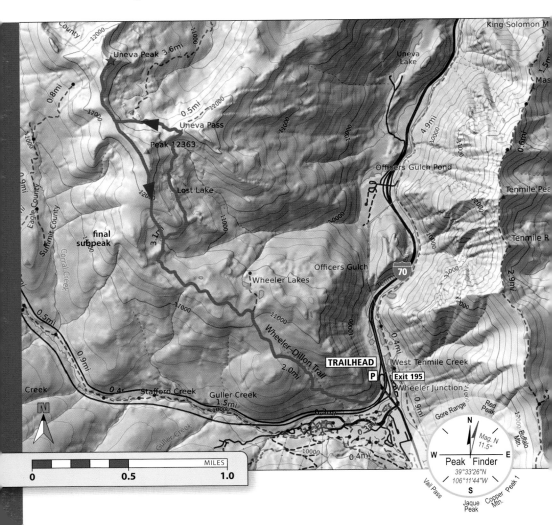

COMMENTS: This hike travels into the beautiful Eagles Nest Wilderness, which is dominated by the rocky backbone of the Gore Range. Uneva Peak lies at the southern tip of the range on the boundary between Eagle and Summit Counties and has more in common with the gentler Tenmile Range, south of the highway, than the sharp peaks that make up the rest of the Gores. There was almost no mining in the range so the area still retains much of its rugged wilderness character. The wildlife has fully recovered from the exploits of Sir St George Gore, an Irish baronet, who devastated the local fauna in the 1850s.

Uneva Lake is located east of the peak and doesn't intersect this hiking route. It was an early recreational area for the residents of Frisco. The Wheeler Lakes are named after Judge John S. Wheeler, a South Park rancher who grazed his cattle in this area.

THE TRAIL: Begin on the trail to the south-southwest and follow the trail with I-70 on the left. After 0.5 mile the trail curves right and ascends northwest across from the Copper Mountain Resort on the left. Higher up keep left at a fork (the right fork leads to the two Wheeler Lakes). The clear trail progresses west, and then curves north, to reach Uneva Pass at 11,900 feet. Uneva Peak will now be visible to the northwest, at the end of a cirque. Proceed west to gain the ridge and then turn north to the summit, marked by a USGS marker and two nearby cairns. The best descent route passes directly to the south-southeast over a grassy ridge. At the final subpeak of this ridge, pass to the left and soon thereafter regain the trail.

Uneva Peak viewed from the pass.

WILD.
AREA

89 Bandit Peak 12,444 Feet

DISTANCE: 5.0 miles on ascent, 3.2 miles on descent

STARTING ELEVATION: 9,248 feet

ELEVATION GAIN: 3,246 feet

HIKING TIME: Up in 214 minutes, down in 122 minutes

TRAIL: Initial 2.25 miles on ascent, final 2.0 miles on descent

SEASON: Late May to mid-October

MAPS: Trails Illustrated #104

NEAREST LANDMARK: Bailey

GETTING THERE: From US-285, 2.7 miles northeast of Bailey or 4.5 miles southwest of Pine Junction, drive north, then northwest, on Park County Road 43 for 8.3 miles to Deer Creek Campground. Then go 0.8 mile farther to a parking area and a trail sign. Park here. En route to this trailhead, take the left fork after 7.0 miles, then the right fork 1.3 miles farther at the campground.

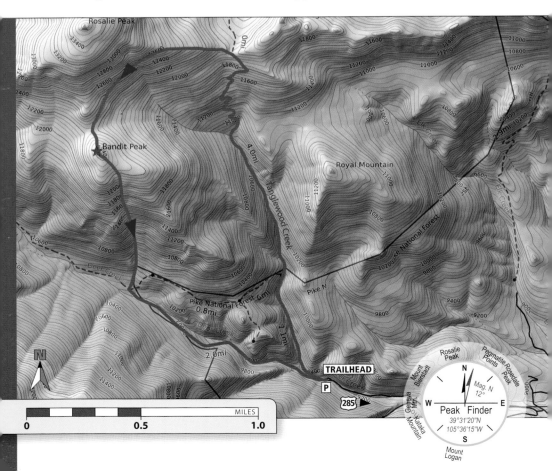

COMMENTS: Bandit Peak is a subpeak of Rosalie Peak, on the southeastern arm of the Mount Evans massif. The southern flanks of Bandit Peak are important winter range for bighorn sheep, as those slopes are often snow free for a good part of the winter. Sheep can usually be spotted in the large open meadows on the south side in spring. By June, they move up the mountain to drop their lambs, then continue to drift higher on the massif. By November, they are back and the echo of crashing horns can sometimes be heard on Bandit Peak.

THE ROUTE: Take the trail to the right, labeled "Tanglewood Trail." (The trail to the left is the Rosalie Trail #603, which ultimately reaches Guanella Pass.) Lose a little elevation and continue northwest along Tanglewood Creek, keeping right at a fork 1.0 mile from the trailhead. After 2.25 miles, the trail reaches a pass at just above treeline, with Mount Rosalie on your left and several rocky knobs, the Pegmatite Points, to your right. (The trail continues north, down to Roosevelt Lakes and Beartrack Lakes.) Leave the pass and the trail by contouring to the west (left), then southwest around a cirque beneath Mount Rosalie for about 1.5 miles, to the north ridge of Bandit Peak. Ascend to the south easily from there, to the cairn on top.

Descend by continuing south over tundra. At a point just above treeline, follow a prominent gully south, down through the trees to meet the Rosalie Trail, paralleling Deer Creek for 1.2 miles. Turn left (east) on Rosalie Trail. It is about 2 miles, and another hour, to complete the loop back to the trailhead.

Looking north to Rosalie Peak from the summit of Bandit Peak.

WILD.
AREA

CMC
CLASSIC
HIKE

90 Kataka Mountain 12,441 Feet

DISTANCE: 5.7 miles on ascent, 3.6 miles on descent

STARTING ELEVATION: 9,610 feet

ELEVATION GAIN: 3,031 feet (includes 200 feet extra)

HIKING TIME: Up in 250 minutes, down in 122 minutes

TRAIL: Initial 4.5 miles on ascent, final 2.1 mile on descent

SEASON: Mid-June to early October

MAPS: Trails Illustrated #104

NEAREST LANDMARK: Grant

GETTING THERE: Either drive north from US-285 at the town of Grant on Park County Road 62 (Guanella Pass Road) for 5.3 miles or drive south from Guanella Pass on Park County Road 62 for 8.1 miles to a parking area on the east side of the road. (Geneva Park is the name given to the meadow on the west side of the road.) Park here.

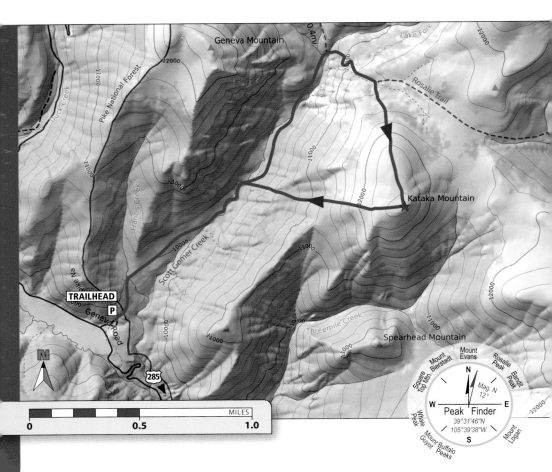

COMMENTS: This gentle, rounded summit in Park County isn't visited frequently, yet it affords wonderful views of Kenosha Pass, South Park, and the surrounding high peaks. The popular fourteeners, Mount Bierstadt and Mount Evans, fill up the horizon to the north. Make this a fall hike, with grand aspen displays along Guanella Pass Road.

Park County, named after South Park, was one of the original territorial counties of Colorado.

Mount Bierstadt (left) and Mount Evans from the summit of Kataka Mountain.

THE ROUTE: The trailhead is well marked, past an open wooden fence by a sign indicating that the intersection for the Rosalie Trail is 4.0 miles and that Abyss Lake is 8.0 miles away. Since this is part of the Mount Evans Wilderness Area, the trail is closed to bicycles and motorized vehicles (but open to horseback travel). Hike northeast on this trail, paralleling Scott Gomer Creek. After 2.1 miles from the trailhead, the trail crosses the creek at a wooden bridge. Another 0.8 mile brings you to another creek crossing, back to the west side.

After about two hours from the trailhead, you reach an open basin and a confluence of Scott Gomer Creek coming from the northwest, with the Lake Fork coming from the northeast. Cross Scott Gomer Creek near the confluence and very quickly the trail reaches a fork. The left fork continues northeast to Abyss Lake. Take the right fork, the Rosalie Trail (which eventually leads to Deer Creek). Continue east on this trail, which rises to timberline after crossing the lake fork. When at about 11,400 feet (just below timberline), where a subpeak of Mount Bierstadt lies directly north, leave the trail and proceed up and south over tundra, past sparse trees. A ridge below the Kataka summit lies to your south. It is about 1.2 miles from the trail, over this ridge, to a small pile of rocks on the flat summit.

For the return, make a loop by proceeding due west, bushwhacking down to regain the trail near the southernmost bridge that crosses Scott Gomer Creek. The trail then returns you southwest to the trailhead.

WILD.
AREA

91 Mount Lady Washington 13,281 Feet

DISTANCE: 5.6 miles on ascent, 4.6 miles on descent (loop)

STARTING ELEVATION: 9,400 feet

ELEVATION GAIN: 4,171 feet (includes 145 feet extra each way)

HIKING TIME: Up in 192 minutes, down in 130 minutes

TRAIL: Initial 5 miles on ascent, final 4 miles on descent

SEASON: July to October

MAPS: Trails Illustrated #200

NEAREST LANDMARK: Meeker Park

GETTING THERE: Drive either 24.8 miles southwest on Colorado 7 from the west end of Lyons or drive 9.5 miles south on Colorado 7 from its junction with US-36 in Estes Park. Then turn west and go 1.1 miles on the paved road to the Longs Peak Ranger Station and park.

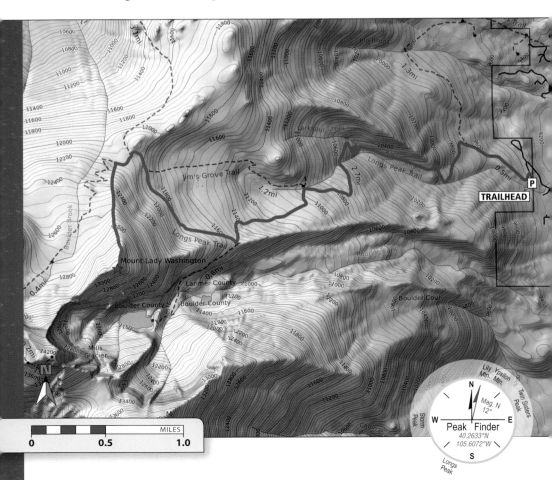

The east face of Longs Peak with Mount Lady Washington on the right.

COMMENTS: The Longs Peak area is very popular with hikers. The trails of Rocky Mountain National Park are impeccably marked and awesome Longs Peak looms above. This is one of several hikes that begin at the Longs Peak Ranger Station. From the top of Mount Lady Washington the view of the east face of Longs Peak is by far the best.

There is no fee for this entry into the National Park but pets, vehicles, and firearms are forbidden on the trails.

THE ROUTE: Start south into the trees from the Ranger Station past a trail register. The excellent trail then turns sharply to the right and arrives at a signed fork 0.5 mile from the trailhead. Go left and soon encounter the flowing waters of Alpine Brook on your left. After 1.8 miles from the trailhead you will cross Larkspur Creek on a bridge with lovely cascades descending on the left. Continue up by trail to another signed fork in another 0.75 mile. Go left, pass timberline, and in another 1.0 mile reach a four-way trail intersection. Straight ahead leads to Chasm Lake but you go right and follow the trail to Longs Peak. Mount Lady Washington lies above on your left. You can scramble directly up to the top but I recommend that you continue on the trail, go left at another signed fork and only leave the trail when you are within 1.0 mile of the Boulderfield and can see the prominent rocky formation that is known as "The Keyhole" to the right of Longs Peak. Then ascend the ridge to the south. It is easy going over rocks and tundra to the small pile of boulders and a register cylinder at the top of Mount Lady Washington. Hopefully the weather is clear since you will never get a better view of massive Longs Peak. On your return I recommend that you carefully work your way down through the rocks to the east and regain the trail about 1.0 mile closer to the trailhead than where you left it.

Comanche Peak 13,277 Feet

DISTANCE: 5.4 miles each way

STARTING ELEVATION: 8,940 feet

ELEVATION GAIN: 4,437 feet (includes 100 extra feet)

HIKING TIME: Up in 214 minutes, down in 142 minutes

TRAIL: All the way

SEASON: Mid-June to early October

MAPS: Trails Illustrated #138

NEAREST LANDMARK: Westcliffe

GETTING THERE: Drive south on CO-69 from Westcliffe at the junction with CO-96 for 3.4 miles. Turn right on Schoolfield Road (Custer County Road 140) and drive for 4.5 miles to a "T." Turn left onto Custer County Road 141. After 1.9 miles, reach an intersection and take the right fork 0.3 mile to the Comanche-Venable trailhead. Regular cars can easily reach this point, 6.75 miles from CO-69.

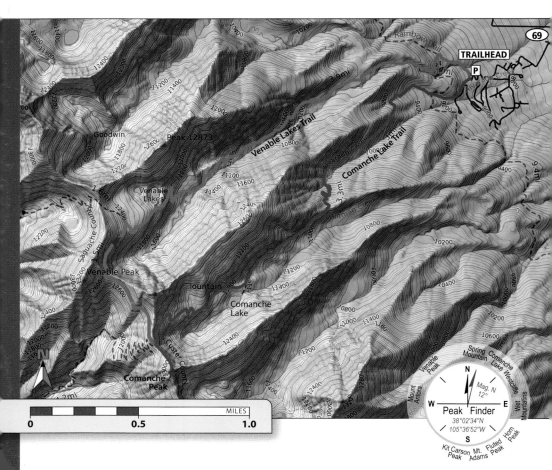

COMMENTS: The very authentic western town of Westcliffe lies in the idyllic Wet Mountain valley, bounded on the west by the Sangre de Cristo Mountains. Formerly called Clifton, the town was re-named by Dr. W. A. Bell after his home-town of Westcliff-on-the-Sea, England.

It is striking how abruptly the Sangre de Cristo Range soars 7,000 feet above the valleys on either side. The Sangres are classic fault-block mountains, situated along massive fault lines. As the range began to thrust upward some 25 million years ago, almost as a single block, the valleys slid down. The actual basement rock is now hidden beneath thousands of feet of sed-iment. Evidence of large earthquakes in the San Luis Valley in recent geologic time indicates continued movement.

Comanche Lake at the base of Comanche Peak.

THE ROUTE: A signed trail at the south-west corner of the parking area rises almost 0.5 mile to reach an intersection with the Rainbow Trail. Proceed to the right on the Rainbow Trail and quickly reach the Comanche Lake Trail on your left. Continue on the Rainbow Trail up the valley to the west. Eventually, Horn Peak comes into view on your left, across the valley. In 3.4 miles on the Rainbow Trail, you will arrive at a point over-looking Comanche Lake, with Comanche Peak looming impressively at the end of the basin. Continue on the trail, rising to the right of the lake in a series of switchbacks, to an unnamed pass at 12,750 feet. Descend about 40 feet from the pass to a saddle on your left. From here, take the faint ridge trail south over tun-dra to the summit and a small cairn. Descend as you ascended.

You may combine this hike with the hike to Venable Peak, descending on the Venable Trail, for a wonderful loop trip through the Sangre de Cristo Wilderness. Retrace your steps to the unnamed pass, then continue on the trail north for 1.0 mile along the west flank of Spring Mountain to another unnamed pass. Pick up the Venable Trail here, following the directions for the Venable Peak hike in reverse to the Rainbow Trail. Turn right (south) at the Rainbow Trail, passing the Comanche Lake Trail in about 0.5 mile. Soon afterwards, turn left (east) to return to your vehicle.

WILD.
AREA

CMC
CLASSIC
HIKE

93 Venable Peak 13,334 Feet

DISTANCE: 6.8 miles each way

STARTING ELEVATION: 8,930 feet

ELEVATION GAIN: 4,404 feet (includes 60 extra feet)

HIKING TIME: Up in 205 minutes, down in 140 minutes

TRAIL: Initial 6.5 miles, off-trail tundra and talus beyond

SEASON: Mid-June to early October

MAPS: Trails Illustrated #138

NEAREST LANDMARK: Westcliffe

GETTING THERE: Drive south on CO-69 from Westcliffe at the junction with CO-96 for 3.4 miles. Turn right on Schoolfield Road (Custer County Road 140) and drive for 4.5 miles to a "T." Turn left onto Custer County Road 141. After 1.9 miles, reach an intersection and take the right fork 0.3 mile to the Comanche-Venable Trailhead. Regular cars can easily reach this point, 6.75 miles from CO-69.

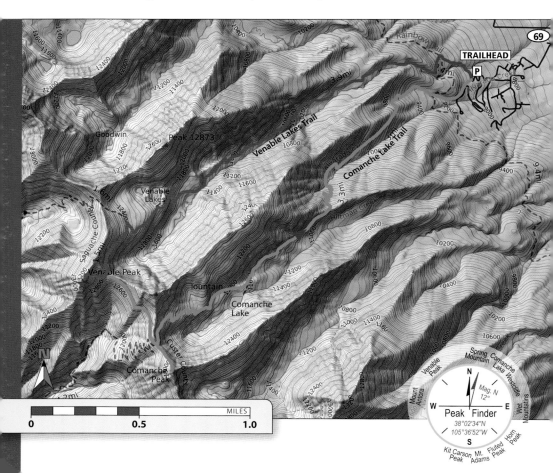

Venable Peak viewed from Comanche Peak. The highest point on the left rises 6 feet above where the ridge connects.

COMMENTS: Part of this hike utilizes the Rainbow Trail, an 85-mile route along the eastern side of the Sangre de Cristo Range. The Abbot's Lodge, passed early in the hike, was owned and operated by the Benedictine Order for many years as a summer camp, and as a support structure for the Holy Cross Abbey, a high school for boys in Cañon City. Venable Pass is not traversed in this route. It lies to the west of the Venable Lakes. Link this route with the Comanche Peak hike for an outstanding loop trip through the Sangre de Cristo Wilderness.

THE ROUTE: A signed trail at the southwest corner of the parking area rises almost 0.5 mile to reach an intersection with the Rainbow Trail. Proceed to the right on the Rainbow Trail, and in less than 0.5 mile, take the left fork at a sign, "Venable Lakes 5 miles." Continue southwest up the valley, with Venable Creek on your left. (A short side trail goes off left to Venable Falls.) Continue on the main trail until it forks at an abandoned cabin. Take the left fork leading to one of the Venable Lakes and soon thereafter to a signed fork. Take the left fork, rising southwest toward the unnamed pass by way of a narrow shelf with steep drop-offs, known as the Phantom Terrace. At the pass, there is no sign. Leave the trail and ascend the ridge to the northwest, curving south to the summit cairn.

You may combine this hike with the Comanche Peak Trail. Retrace your steps to the unnamed pass, then continue on the trail south for 1.0 mile, and along the west flank of Spring Mountain, to another unnamed pass. Pick up the Comanche Trail here, following the Comanche Peak hike in reverse to the Rainbow Trail. Turn right (south) at the Rainbow Trail, then soon turn left (east) to return to your vehicle.

WILD.
AREA

CMC
CLASSIC
HIKE

94 Mount Logan 12,871 Feet

DISTANCE: 9.2 miles on ascent, 4.55 miles on descent

STARTING ELEVATION: 9,320 feet

ELEVATION GAIN: 4,145 feet (includes 350 extra feet)

HIKING TIME: Up in 240 minutes, down in 130 minutes

TRAIL: Initial 8.2 miles on ascent, final 2.0 miles on descent

SEASON: Mid-June to early October

MAPS: Trails Illustrated #104

NEAREST LANDMARK: Bailey

GETTING THERE: From US-285, 2.7 miles northeast of Bailey or 4.5 miles southwest of Pine Junction, drive north, then northwest, on Park County Road 43 for 8.3 miles to Deer Creek Campground. Then go 0.8 mile farther to a parking area and a trail sign. Park here. (En route to this trailhead, take the left fork after 7.0 miles, then the right fork 1.3 miles farther at the campground.)

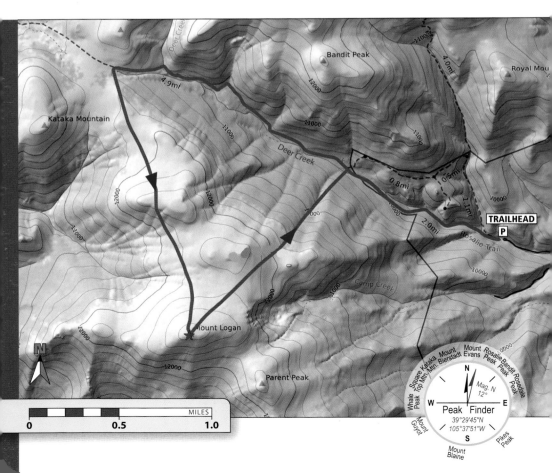

COMMENTS: Mount Logan, like the Colorado county of the same name, was named after John Alexander Logan, an Illinois politician and a Union General in the Civil War. He inaugurated the national holiday of Memorial Day.

This big peak is infrequently climbed, a condition that seems to suit a large band of bighorn sheep. Locals in the town of Grant share their backyards with them in winter, but come summer, the sheep are back up on Logan's rolling tundra slopes.

Don't count on many trail markers as you approach the summit of Mount Logan.

THE ROUTE: Go west a few hundred yards to some trail signs and a fork. Take the left fork, the Rosalie Trail. Follow it west and northwest, along Deer Creek and crossing it several times, for 5.8 miles to a ridge and a junction with the Threemile Creek Trail, #635 in the Mount Evans Wilderness. Follow the Threemile Creek Trail as it curves south, upward between Kataka Mountain on your right (west) and subpeaks of Mount Logan on your left (east). The trail becomes rather faint. Leave the trail near treeline, going southeast up the subpeak of Mount Logan, keeping to the right of its highpoint. At the ridge, the true summit becomes visible to the south. Continue over tundra, losing 244 feet as you make directly for the highpoint. From the Threemile Creek cutoff at the Rosalie Trail, it is 3.1 miles to the top of Mount Logan, where there is a large ring of rocks, some old wooden planks, and a Colorado Mountain Club register cylinder.

WILD.
AREA

To descend, hike over tundra and rocks to the northeast. At the most easterly subpeak, enter the trees and bushwhack through a moderately dense forest, keeping northeast to regain the Rosalie Trail. A creek becomes evident after you enter the trees. Keep this creek to your left, following it to the junction with Deer Creek. Pick up the trail here and hike 2.0 miles east to your vehicle. (If you dislike bushwhacking, descend the same way you came up. This will add 4.65 miles to the hike.)

95 South Twin Cone Peak 12,323 Feet

DISTANCE: 7.0 miles each way

STARTING ELEVATION: 8,293 feet

ELEVATION GAIN: 4,130 feet (includes 100 extra feet)

HIKING TIME: Up in 265 minutes, down in 183 minutes

TRAIL: Initial 5.5 miles, tundra walk beyond

SEASON: Early June to mid-October

MAPS: Trails Illustrated #104 & 105

NEAREST LANDMARK: Grant

GETTING THERE: On US-285 from the town of Grant, either drive 2.1 miles west of the Shawnee Post Office or drive 2.7 miles east of the Camp Santa Maria entrance and park near a Ben Tyler Trail sign. There is parking on the south side of the highway.

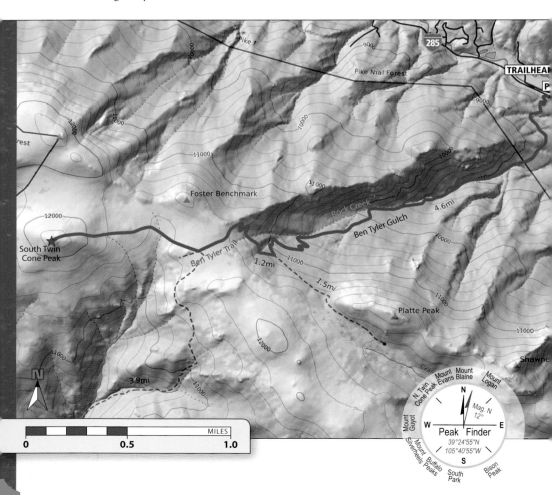

South Twin Cone Peak from the southeast.

COMMENTS: This is one of the Platte River Mountains, visible from South Park around the town of Jefferson. Mount Blaine, 1.0 mile north, and North Twin Cone Peak, 1.3 miles northwest, can readily be reached over tundra and talus from this peak. At treeline are some examples of krummholz (a German word meaning "crooked wood"), wind-tortured dwarf conifers that survive in this severe environment. You may also observe a few "banner trees," with branches only on the leeward sides. The fierce, westerly prevailing winds strip any growth off the windward sides.

This is another wonderful hike in the fall season, with colorful, fallen aspen leaves blanketing the upper half of the Ben Tyler Trail. These trees are evidence of a fire that swept the gulch less than half a century ago. This group changes to identical shades of red and gold in unison around mid-September, evidence that they are clones, or individual trees sprouting from the same root system.

THE ROUTE: Begin up the trail to the west-southwest. After 2.7 miles take a left fork and after 1.7 miles more take the right fork to Rock Creek. Another 0.6 mile brings you to the ridge at treeline. Leave the trail and hike to the right (west) across marshes, willows, and krummholz past a false summit to a cairn and pole atop South Twin Cone Peak. Descend by the same route.

96 Antora Peak 13,269 Feet

DISTANCE: 6.5 miles each way

STARTING ELEVATION: 10,886 feet

ELEVATION GAIN: 4,423 feet (includes 1,020 feet extra each way)

HIKING TIME: Up in 245 minutes, down in 210 minutes

TRAIL: Initial 5.5 miles, off-trail tundra and talus beyond

SEASON: Mid-June to early October

MAPS: Trails Illustrated #139

NEAREST LANDMARK: Salida

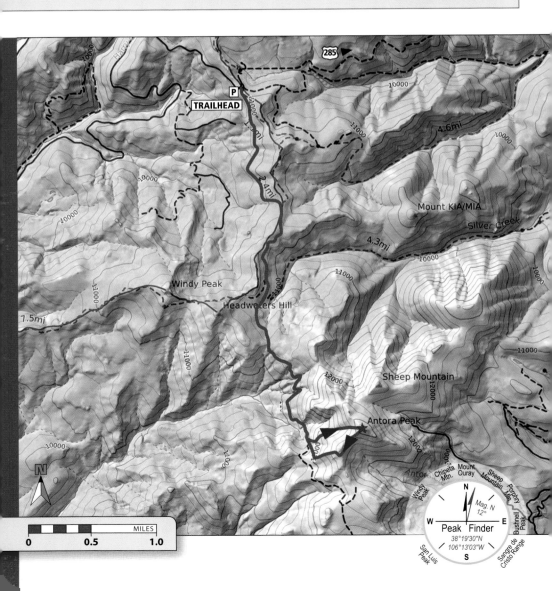

GETTING THERE: From west of Salida at the junction of US-50 and US-285, drive south toward Poncha Pass for 5.2 miles. Turn right onto Chaffee County Road 200. This dirt road can be readily negotiated by regular cars all the way to Marshall Pass. Follow Chaffee County Road 200 for 2.35 miles and turn right onto County Road 202. Ascend for 0.9 mile and turn right onto County Road 200 again. In 10.85 miles from US-285, Marshall Pass (10,846 feet) will be reached. Just past the sign on the pass, turn left and shortly reach a four-way intersection. Park around here. Marshall Pass can also be reached from the west via the tiny settlement of Sargents on US-50.

COMMENTS: Marshall Pass was discovered by Army Lieutenant William L. Marshall, part of the Wheeler Survey team. The pass was first a wagon then a railroad route between Gunnison and Salida. Climbers know Antora Peak as the southern terminus of the mighty Sawatch Range.

A portion of this hike follows both the Colorado Trail and the Continental Divide National Scenic Trail, which are collinear in this area. Elk can be abundant.

Antora Peak from the west.

THE ROUTE: Begin south on an excellent road, part of the Colorado Trail. In about five minutes, pass through a gate, blocking the road to vehicles. Antora Peak will be visible ahead. Lose some elevation and in about 25 minutes from the gate, take the left fork, leading upward and generally south. Within 15 minutes, you pass through a fence and encounter a trail sign. Continue south. In 1.0 mile, reach signs that indicate you are on the Divide Trail and that the Silver Creek Trail drops down to the east. The trail continues south, and within another half hour, cuts up into trees, passing through a barbed wire fence. Leave the main trail and follow this fence to the east, directly toward Antora Peak. A faint trail passes alongside this fence at times. Within another half hour, you will reach a gate through the fence and a definite trail leading south from the gate. Follow this trail as it curves around the western flank of Antora Peak. At a second creek crossing, reached in about twenty minutes, leave the trail and ascend to the east along the mostly dry creek bed into a steep talus and possibly snow-filled gulch above timberline. Continue east, over loose rock at times, to a ridge leading over a few false summits. Finally, reach a small cairn, an animal skull, and two rock shelters at the top.

For the descent, take the same general route, but instead, take the ridge to your left. This ridge runs east to west and it will enable you to descend over mostly tundra, reaching the snow-filled gulch at a lower level. Then continue ba⬛⬛⬛⬛⬛⬛⬛⬛⬛⬛⬛oute.

WILD.
AREA

97 Mount Antero 14,269 Feet

DISTANCE: 8.3 miles each way

STARTING ELEVATION: 9,420 feet

ELEVATION GAIN: 4,919 feet (includes 35 extra feet each way)

HIKING TIME: Up in 250 minutes, down in 175 minutes

TRAIL: All the way

SEASON: July to October

MAPS: Trails Illustrated #130

NEAREST LANDMARK: Buena Vista

GETTING THERE: From the junction of US-24 and US-285 south of Buena Vista, drive south on US-285 for 5.5 miles and turn right (west) onto Chaffee County Road 162. Follow Road 162 for 12.0 miles to the Baldwin Gulch Road on your left and park. This point lies west of Alpine and east of Saint Elmo.

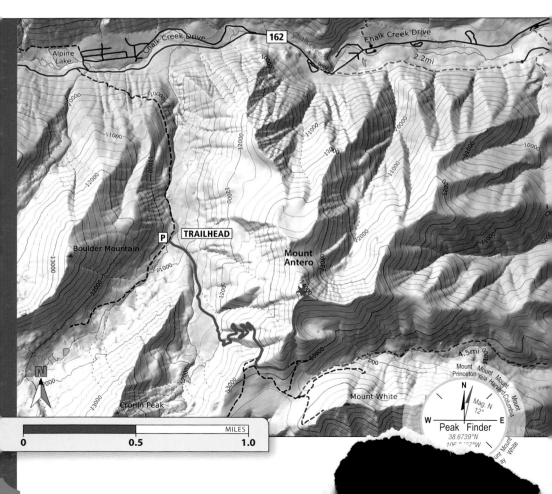

The view of Mount Antero from Baldwin Lake.

COMMENTS: Mount Antero is the tenth highest fourteener in Colorado and has a reputation for containing many gemstones. A four-wheel drive road extends to within 0.8 mile of the summit. Many hikers will drive up this road for 2.8 miles and park just before the road crosses Baldwin Creek and save 1,425 feet of elevation gain. This hike description, however, begins at Road 162 where the four-wheel drive road begins.

THE ROUTE: Begin southeast up the rough road and follow it for 2.8 miles to a fork and a sign. Take the left fork and cross Baldwin Creek, pass timberline, and ascend a series of switchbacks as you approach Mount Antero in a counter-clockwise direction. After 6.3 miles from the trailhead, take a foot trail to the left of the road up to a ridge. The foot trail reconnects with the road near a fork. Go left and follow the road up to the east. After 0.3 more miles, take another left fork that leads up to the end of the four-wheel drive road with Mount

Antero now visible to the north. From the road end, follow the clear trail on the southeast side of the ridge steeply up to a cairn, two rock shelters, and a register at the top. Avoid shortcuts on your way back.

…aching …

ick by way of your ascent ro

The view of Mount Antero from Baldwin Lake.

98 Mount Sopris 12,953 Feet
West Mount Sopris 12,953 Feet

DISTANCE: 6.0 miles each way

STARTING ELEVATION: 8,600 feet

ELEVATION GAIN: 5,089 feet (includes 736 ft. extra between peaks)

HIKING TIME: Up in 285 minutes, down in 225 minutes

TRAIL: All the way

SEASON: Mid-June to early October

MAPS: Trails Illustrated #128 or 143

NEAREST LANDMARK: Carbondale

GETTING THERE: Drive south on CO-133 from the junction with CO-82 at Carbondale for 2.8 miles and turn left onto a paved road with a stop sign. This is Garfield County Road 111 (changing to Pitkin County Road 5), which follows

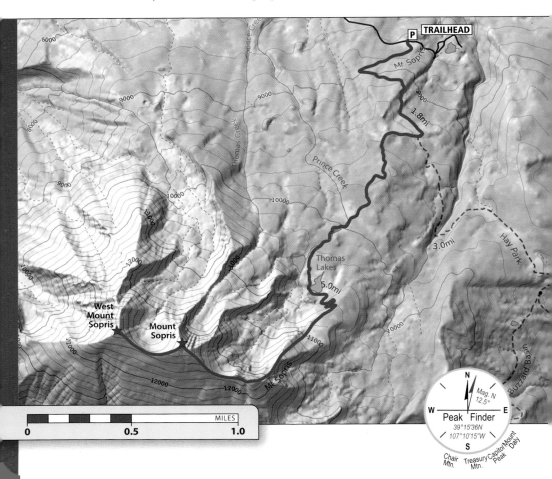

Prince Creek to the southeast. After 1.6 miles on this road, take the right fork, around where the pavement ends. Drive 4.8 miles farther and again take a right fork. In 2.0 more miles, you arrive at the trailhead and parking area. A barrier prevents all vehicular access to the trail from this point. (The road end is 0.4 mile farther at Dinkle Lake.)

COMMENTS: These two peaks are 0.8 mile apart and, interestingly, of identical height. Due to the absence of any nearby mountains of comparable height, Mount Sopris dominates the skyline southeast from the towns of Glenwood Springs and Carbondale. It is a surprisingly gentle giant, surrounded by the rugged beauty of the Elk Range. Sitting at the far west end of the Elks (one of the few east-west trending ranges in the United States), one can see the stark contrast between the deep red sedimentary formations of the eastern end and the almost-white intrusive rocks of the western peaks.

The mountain is named after Captain Richard Sopris, who explored the area in 1860, discovered Glenwood Springs and later, in Denver, began City Park and became mayor.

THE ROUTE: Hike southeast and then south about 1.3 miles to a fork. (The left route goes to Hay Park and West Sopris Creek.) Take the right fork, going west and then southwest, for 2.0 more miles to Thomas Lakes. From between the southeastern and the southwestern lakes, a trail leads south up a steep, vegetated ridge. Take this route, keep to the left of the talus, pass timberline and rise to the main east-west ridge. Keep on the trail as it turns west (right) up this ridge and crosses a false 12,453-foot summit en route to the Mount Sopris summit cairn. West Mount Sopris lies 0.8 mile and about 30 minutes to the west over tundra and talus. There is a register and cairn at its summit. Follow the same trail back to the trailhead.

CMC
CLASSIC
HIKE

Mount Sopris. (David Hite)

99 Iowa Peak 13,831 Feet

DISTANCE: 7.0 miles each way

STARTING ELEVATION: 9,669 feet

ELEVATION GAIN: 4,962 feet (includes 400 feet extra each way)

HIKING TIME: Up in 298 minutes, down in 197 minutes

TRAIL: Initial 5.6 miles, off-trail tundra and talus beyond

SEASON: Late June to early October

MAPS: Trails Illustrated #129

NEAREST LANDMARK: Buena Vista

GETTING THERE: Either drive south on US-24 for 19.7 miles from Leadville or drive 15.3 miles north from the traffic light in Buena Vista. Just south of the small settlement of Granite, and north of the Clear Creek Reservoir, a clearly marked dirt road, Chaffee County Road 390, goes 7.9 miles west to the remains

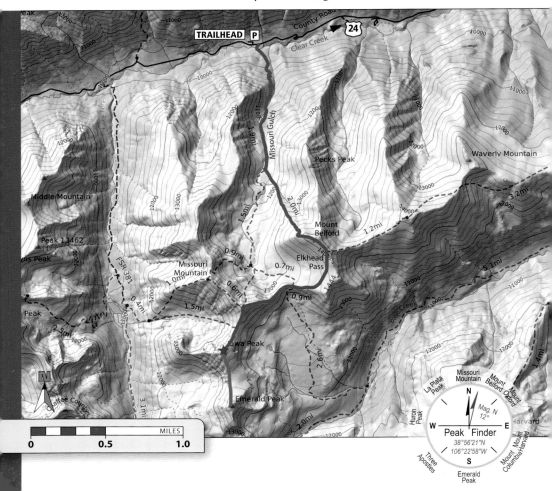

of Vicksburg. At Vicksburg, park in the fenced parking area on the south side of the road. Regular cars can come this far with no difficulty. (The road continues west-southwest, past Rockdale and Winfield, to an eventual dead end.)

COMMENTS: The ghost town of Vicksburg was originally occupied from 1881 to 1885. Named after Vick Keller, an early resident, the town once had two hotels and a school. Only a small museum remains.

Nearby Emerald Peak is well named, as Missouri Basin is a spectacular tundra garden filled to the brim with summer wildflowers. Ringed by a dozen summits, including four fourteeners, it is one of the largest alpine basins in the Sawatch Range. But the long, arduous trail up Pine Creek keeps it blissfully uncrowded.

THE ROUTE: Follow the trail south from the parking area, cross Clear Creek on a bridge and soon, on the left, pass the grave of Baby Huffman, a miner's child who died at one month of age many years ago. Continue steeply up the trail into Missouri Gulch, eventually running alongside the creek. After one hour from the trailhead, reach an abandoned cabin

Looking down the Missouri Basin. (Eric Wiseman)

on your left. Continue up into the basin as two fourteeners come into view—Mount Belford on your left (east) and Missouri Mountain on your right (west). Continue on the trail above timberline, and in about 130 minutes from the abandoned cabin, reach Elkhead Pass at 13,220 feet. Ahead of you lies Missouri Basin and Mount Harvard. Iowa Peak also comes into view to the southwest, with Emerald Peak on its left (south). Continue on the trail southward, down about 400 feet from Elkhead Pass. Leave the trail when you see a clear, gradual route to the Iowa Peak–Missouri Mountain saddle. The saddle will be reached in about 96 minutes from the pass. Then turn left (south), ascending over easy tundra and talus in twelve minutes to the non-descript Iowa Peak summit.

Emerald Peak is an easy ridge walk to the south if you have the time and energy. Descend by your ascent route.

WILD.
AREA

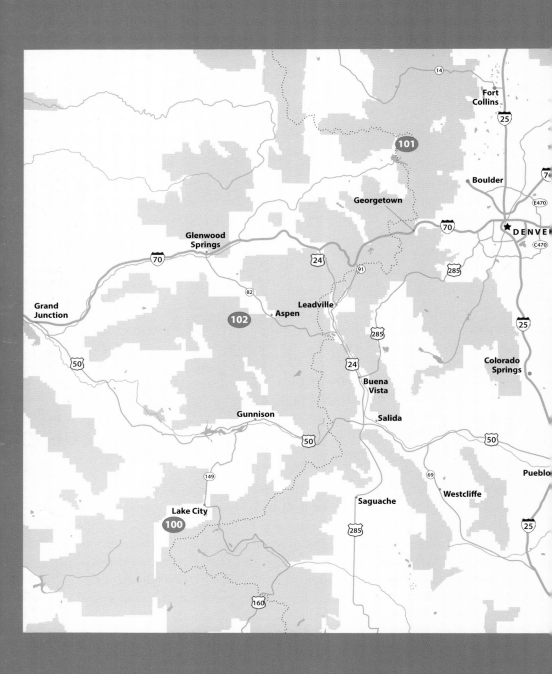

100 Engineer Mountain 13,218 Feet

DISTANCE: 9.1 miles each way

STARTING ELEVATION: 8,854 feet

ELEVATION GAIN: 4,364 feet

HIKING TIME: Up in 360 minutes, down in 240 minutes

TRAIL: All the way

SEASON: Mid-June to early October

MAPS: Trails Illustrated #141

NEAREST LANDMARK: Ouray

GETTING THERE: Drive south from Ouray on US-550 (the Million Dollar Highway) for 3.4 miles to a cutoff to the east, marked with a stop sign, an Ouray County Road 18 sign, and an Engineer Mountain Road sign, with recommendations for four-wheel drive. Park here at the start of this road. (If you are able

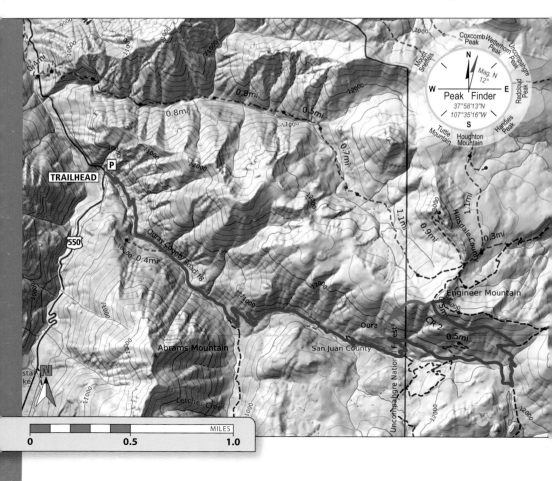

The view of Coxcomb (left), Wetterhorn (center), and Uncompaghre (right) from the summit of Engineer Mountain. Right: Engineer Mountain from the pass.

to drive your vehicle up this rough road, it will decrease the distance, time, and elevation gain listed for this hike accordingly. High clearance is essential and four-wheel drive will be needed on occasion.)

COMMENTS: Engineer Mountain is a name also given to other Colorado peaks. This peak lies just south of the Engineer Pass route, built in 1877 by Otto Mears to carry stagecoaches and wagons between Lake City on the east and Ouray and Silverton on the west. The original Engineer Pass was located closer to the Engineer Mountain summit and was steeper.

THE ROUTE: Proceed up the road, taking the left fork at 2.3 miles. (The right fork leads into Poughkeepsie Gulch.) After 2.7 more miles, again take the left fork. (The right fork goes to Mineral Point.) In 1.9 miles farther, continue again on the left fork. (The right fork leads south to Animas Forks and Cinnamon Pass.) By a series of switchbacks, you will reach the high point of this road in 1.9 miles from the last fork. At this highest point, leave the main road and ascend to the east-southeast via an old mining road for 0.3 mile to the summit, marked by a metal rod embedded in a rock. Return as you ascended. (The main road continues north for 0.4 mile to Engineer Pass and a large sign. The road then drops down into Henson Gulch, ending at Lake City.)

The road can be a dusty affair on weekends, when it is popular with four-wheel drive enthusiasts. You can shorten your return by heading due west off the summit of Engineer Mountain. Follow the ridge down for 1.0 mile, then pick up an old road that switchbacks south into a gulley, past old mines and prospects, to intercept Engineer Mountain Road.

101 Pagoda Mountain 13,497 Feet

DISTANCE: 6.2 miles each way

STARTING ELEVATION: 8,380 feet

ELEVATION GAIN: 5,177 feet (includes 60 extra feet)

HIKING TIME: Up in 375 minutes, down in 278 minutes

TRAIL: Initial 3.0 miles, only intermittent and faint trail beyond

SEASON: Late June to early October

MAPS: Trails Illustrated #200; Rocky Mountain National Park map

NEAREST LANDMARK: Allenspark

GETTING THERE: Drive 2.2 miles north of Allenspark or 1.1 miles south of Meeker Park on CO-7. Take the paved road going southwest for 0.4 mile and make a right turn onto a dirt road that leads to Copeland Lake and the Wild Basin Ranger Station. Pay a fee and park in the designated area within 100 yards on your right. This is the Sandbeach Lake Trailhead, your starting point.

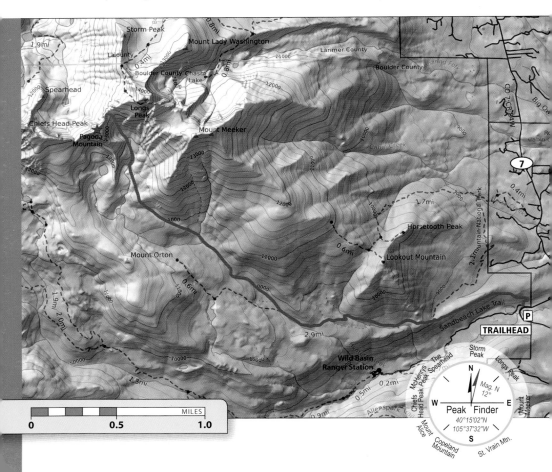

COMMENTS: Pagoda Mountain is named after the prominent configuration of its summit, seen on clear days from the Boulder and Denver areas as the peak to the left of Longs Peak.

From the summit, there are panoramic views into aptly named Wild Basin, as well as a front row seat for watching the masses toil up the "Homestretch" on Longs Peak. In contrast, you are likely to enjoy Pagoda's fine summit all to yourself!

Pagoda Mountain.

THE ROUTE: Proceed northwest to the right of Copeland Lake for 100 yards to a sign and the Sandbeach Lake trailhead. The trail begins steeply to the northwest, and then curves west for about 3.0 miles to a point where Hunters Creek, flowing from the northwest, crosses the trail. This junction will be reached in about 90 minutes. Leave the Sandbeach Lake Trail and angle obliquely to the northwest following Hunters Creek, keeping it on your left. After about 1.3 miles along Hunters Creek, reach a junction of two branches of the creek. Cross this junction, continue northwest and leave the creeks.

Stay close to the base of Mount Meeker, lying to the right. Pagoda Mountain will now be visible. Continue eventually in a more northerly direction, often over rocks, and up into a couloir with talus, scree, and some loose footing. Ascend this to the saddle, which lies between Pagoda Mountain to the west (left) and Longs Peak to the east (right). From the saddle, turn west and ascend steeply over boulders to a summit cairn and a register cylinder. Some easy hand work is necessary between the saddle and the top, but the footing is quite solid. Return the same way you ascended.

102 Capitol Peak 14,130 Feet

DISTANCE: 8.12 miles each way

STARTING ELEVATION: 9,420 feet

ELEVATION GAIN: Day 1: 2,660 feet; Day 2: 3,000 feet (includes 475 feet extra each way); Total 5,660 feet

HIKING TIME: Day 1: 197 minutes to base camp; Day 2: up in 218 minutes, down to base camp in 188 minutes, base camp to trailhead in 162 minutes.

TRAIL: All the way, but with moderate/difficult scrambling near top

SEASON: Early July to late September

MAPS: Trails Illustrated #128

NEAREST LANDMARK: Snowmass

GETTING THERE: Drive north from the Castle Creek bridge in Aspen on CO-82 for 13.8 miles or drive south from Glenwood Springs on CO-82 for 23 miles. At the Snowmass Post Office and a service station on the south side of the road, turn south along Snowmass Creek for 1.8 miles to a "T." Turn right and drive southwest. After 4.9 miles from the "T," the road paving ends. Continue on the dirt road for 3.4 more miles to the road end, in a grove of aspen trees. A sign marks the trail on your left. Park here. The road is steep and rough in spots over the last mile. A high-clearance vehicle or four-wheel drive may be required in certain years or after a storm.

COMMENTS: This is the most strenuous hike in this guide, but also the most spectacular. Climbers consider this classic fourteener to be one of the most challenging peaks, famous for its exposed ridge. While it has been done in a

Capitol Peak from the north.

day, you will want to take two or three days with an idyllic camp below Capitol Lake. Capitol Peak and nearby Snowmass Mountain were called "The Twins" or the "Capitol" and the "Whitehouse" by earlier residents of the area.

THE ROUTE: From the trailhead there is a lovely view of Capitol Peak at the end of the basin. Hike down and south on the excellent trail. You will lose 380 feet en route to a crossing of Capitol Creek via a large tree trunk. (The crossing may be difficult in June due to high water.) The trail then rises, crossing Capitol Creek a few more times. The trail is not steadily upward; occasionally it loses elevation. After more than 6.0 miles, arrive at a flat, tree-covered area just at timberline, to the right of the trail. This makes a good campsite. Several hundred yards

The Knife Edge on Capitol Peak.

farther south lies Capitol Lake, often frozen well into July.

The next morning, continue south on the trail, which soon forks. Continue steeply up and east to the saddle between Mount Daly on the left and Capitol Peak on the right. From this saddle, the trail proceeds south, high along the eastern flanks of Capitol Peak's north ridge. The trail at this point is marked by cairns and follows a series of ledges. Some use of hands may be necessary, but the exposure is usually slight. Eventually a talus slope is reached. Cross this to gain the summit of a subpeak at 13,664 feet called K-2. The Capitol Peak summit will now be visible to the southwest across a rocky ridge. Descend from K-2 toward this ridge, to a narrow section known as the "Knife Edge." This famous spot, about 60 feet long, is best traversed by straddling. The rock is solid enough, but the drop-offs on both sides are quite abrupt and lengthy. In good weather, this crossing can readily be made, although with care. (This is not a good place to be if lightning is approaching!) Once beyond the Knife Edge, continue scrambling north along the ridge for 150 yards, then traverse left out onto the main face. The trail then continues by way of cairn-marked ledges in a clockwise direction to the summit cairn and a Colorado Mountain Club register cylinder.

After returning back across the Knife Edge, you may avoid the rocky ledges between K-2 and the Mount Daly–K-2 saddle by dropping more easterly from

WILD.
AREA

CMC
CLASSIC
HIKE

Illustration by Jesse Crock

Join Today.
Adventure Tomorrow.

The Colorado Mountain Club helps you maximize living in an outdoor playground and connects you with other adventure-loving mountaineers. We summit 14ers, climb rock faces, work to protect the mountain experience, and educate generations of Coloradans.